Students and Teachers Writing Together:
Perspectives on Journal Writing

JOY KREEFT PEYTON

Editor

Typeset in Aster by
WorldComp, Sterling, Virginia
and printed by
Pantagraph Printing, Bloomington, Illinois

Director of Publications: Helen Kornblum
Publications Assistant: Rosanna Landis

Library of Congress Catalog No. 89-051728
ISBN 0-939791-36-6

To Jana and Leslee,
who first sparked my interest in interactive writing

Contents

Acknowledgments

This book grew out of a TESOL Colloquium on journal writing arranged by Donna Jurich and Lauren Vanett. Donna originally had the idea that the presentations could become a book, and we are happy to see the project finally come to fruition. We are particularly grateful to Diane Larsen-Freeman for her encouragement and support of this publication, and to the students who opened their journals to us and were willing to spend time talking with us about their writing.

Introduction

Most of us have experienced the frustration of encountering a telephone answering machine rather than the person we were hoping to talk to. Instead of the conversation we want to have, we hear a "canned" speech—and are asked to respond in kind. While facilitating communication in the long run, this electronic answering service is a poor substitute for live person-to-person interaction.

Students must feel similarly frustrated when they write for their classes. Instead of receiving thoughtful responses to their ideas, they too often read canned replies: "This is an interesting paper, but you need to work on . . . ". Writing thus becomes an obligatory classroom exercise for students and teachers—students hoping to complete assignments successfully and meet the teacher's expectations, teachers attempting to give students instructive feedback without spending an hour on each paper. We all recognize that such interaction has only limited value for promoting learning and the improvement of students' writing abilities. How can teachers, then, ensure that students' experiences with writing involve them in meaningful communication and foster their language development?

In attempting to address this question, the authors in this volume have explored the use of journal writing in classes for nonnative English speakers and deaf students,[1] a type of written interaction between teachers and students that focuses on meaning rather than form and is a means of developing students' linguistic competence, their understanding of course content, and their ability to communicate in written English.[2] The work with journal writing reported here addresses several issues of concern to all writing teachers:

- how to engage students so that they write meaningful papers that communicate their ideas;
- how to respond to students' writing in ways that encourage them to explore and develop not only their writing skills but also their language skills;
- how to develop writing syllabi that will help students succeed in other courses and in future writing tasks in English;

- how to integrate journal writing with current theories of curriculum design so that it both fits into established curriculum and influences curriculum development;
- how to follow students' writing progress on both the discourse and the grammatical levels.

The need to relate journal writing to larger curricular issues is indeed pressing, for without the knowledge of students' personal goals, needs, and struggles, the most carefully designed curriculum can remain irrelevant to their lives. One current approach to curriculum design focuses on the notion of "reconceptualizaton," i.e., the constant examination of assumptions and values by both teachers and students (see Meath-Lang, Chapter 1, this volume). The journal writing described in this volume engages participants in just such a process. The exchange between teachers and students involves a mutual search for meaning in personally relevant content, whether in developing an understanding of a novel or essay or mastering the basic skills of writing a comprehensible text. In communicating actively and honestly in journal exchanges, teachers explore and examine their educational and personal philosophies and assumptions as they grapple with how to respond to the students' writing and to the students themselves. At the same time, students examine their assumptions and reflect on their lives and on what they are learning as they untangle their ideas of literature, writing, and their own experiences.

In its focus on exploration, meaning, and honest exchange, journal writing promotes students' "communicative competence," a concept fundamental to second language curriculum design (see Savignon, 1983, for example). Indeed, the importance of the role of communicative competence in second-language education has become so "widely accepted . . . that most programs could be said to incorporate some elements" of it (Bowen, Madsen, & Hilferty, 1985, p. 49–50). The concept of communicative competence takes into account social factors related to learning rather than focusing solely on linguistic competence, as earlier approaches to language teaching have done. Through its emphasis on content and interaction rather than on the linguistic and organizational forms of writing, journal writing allows teachers to follow the principles of communicative competence, teaching social and cultural norms for the use of language, not simply its forms.

A related issue, more narrowly focused on the individual writing classroom, is how to engage students in writing that is meaningful and communicative. Journal writing, in which students write about themselves and about ideas and issues of concern to them, fulfills that goal by involving students in authentic communication with a reader who responds primarily to *what* they have communicated rather than *how* they have communicated.

The student journals described here consist of "original, student-generated material" (Taylor, 1981, p. 11) in that the students selected the content. In the journals in which students explored their reactions to pieces of literature as well as in those in which they described their own lives, they wrote about what interested and concerned them, not about predetermined topics assigned by the teacher. They had to decide not how to present the teacher's ideas but how to choose and then express their own, a rare phenomenon in stark contrast to most writing assignments, which, unfortunately, neither "provide an opportunity for students to communicate ideas of serious interest to them" nor require "any commitment" from them (Taylor, 1981, p. 9). In these classes, the students used writing to discover and explore ideas rather than to demonstrate their "mastery of subject area material" or "simple obedience" (Applebee, 1984, p. 170). They were, in effect, granted ownership of the content of their writing, and they developed a heightened interest in what they were communicating and learning and an investment in communicating their ideas clearly.

Eliciting and maintaining students' engagement in writing involves not only what they write about but also how their writing is received and responded to. Studies have shown that teachers most often respond to student writing as evaluators (Britton, Burgess, Martin, McLeod, & Rosen, 1975; Applebee, 1981), responding to form rather than content (Zamel, 1985). Yet this response limits the ways in which students approach writing tasks. Rather than using writing to discover or explore ideas or to engage in dialogue, students must try to produce written text that satisfies the standards by which it will be evaluated. Such evaluation elicits static, "finished" pieces from students, who are concerned with getting a good grade rather than with communicating.

The teachers represented in this volume did not play the "default" role of evaluator of their students' writing; instead, they responded first and foremost as human beings interested in understanding what their students were trying to convey and in communicating their understandings and reactions. They established authentic interaction with their students, avoiding the common "Interesting ideas, but . . . " evaluative response. They made their responses comprehensible, at the same time stretching their students' thinking and language skills by asking them to consider other ideas and points of view and by using language slightly beyond the students' levels of proficiency (i.e., interacting with students within their "zones of proximal development" [Vygotsky, 1962]). Through their written responses, these teachers encouraged their students to become engaged in written interaction and invested in the content and direction of that interaction. The students were empowered by having teachers respond to their lives and ideas authentically and respectfully.

The students were not alone in their engagement with the journal writing and with their audiences; the teachers in the classes described in this volume became writers as well. By writing journals themselves in addition to responding to the content of their students' writing, Vanett and Jurich became "collaborators" (Applebee, 1984) in the writing process with their students, coming to be seen as friends as well as teachers. In her literature class for deaf students, Walworth became involved in negotiating with them the meanings of texts that they read, encouraging them to explore and at times to revise their understandings. Meath-Lang engaged herself and her students in explorations and examinations of their lives and their ideas, that is, in "a process of discovery" (Zamel, 1982, p. 206). The teacher in Peyton's study provided an ongoing model of thought and self-expression in English in her responses to student entries. Albertini gave feedback to students about the textual quality of their writing as well as models of cohesive text. In all of these classes, the students experienced the give-and-take of writing for an authentic audience and, in return, of being expected to respond as an authentic audience for the teacher's writing.

Having established that journal writing addresses issues of concern to teachers and educational theorists, we now must ask: Do students actually learn from engaging in journal writing? The answer is that, despite some difficulties for some students (see Lucas, Chapter 6), journal writing has several positive effects on students that can enhance their performances not only in the journal writing itself but also in other courses and in other writing tasks. In Vanett's and Jurich's classes, students increased their confidence in their ability to write in English and to improve that ability (see Lucas), and they developed skills in using various rhetorical modes and sentence structures, gathering information to support a thesis, and arguing issues from different points of view (see Vanett and Jurich, Chapter 2). Albertini's students learned about one element of good writing, the production of cohesive text, and were empowered by the awareness that they already possessed many of the skills necessary to be good writers. Peyton's results indicate that journal writing allows students to develop their facility with written English as their oral language develops; the writing of the nonnative-English-speaking students in her study serves as a record of their patterns of acquisition of English morphological forms. Walworth's literature students developed the skill of integrating their background knowledge with the texts that ·they were reading, an important skill in all reading contexts. Students in all of these classes developed their abilities to reflect—on themselves, their own lives, their assumptions, and their learning—and to comprehend and use written English.

The volume is organized around three different issues in journal writing: its relation to curriculum theory, its classroom uses, and its implications for learning. In Chapter 1, "The Dialogue Journal: Reconceiving Curriculum and Teaching," Bonnie Meath-Lang explains that the use of dialogue journals creates a student-centered curriculum involving dialogue. She examines the dialogue journal writing of deaf students and their teacher in the context of current curriculum theory and describes ways in which both teachers and students are encouraged to examine their perceptions, knowledge, and concerns through this writing.

Three papers focus on the uses of journal writing in the classroom. In Chapter 2, "The Missing Link: Connecting Journal Writing to Academic Writing," Lauren Vanett and Donna Jurich argue that journal writing can be a tool to teach the writing skills needed in a variety of contexts, including school and business. They discuss techniques for helping students transfer the skills they exhibit in their personal writing to more formal writing. Margaret Walworth also uses journal writing as a teaching tool in her literature classes for deaf students. In Chapter 3, "Interactive Teaching of Reading: A Model," she shows through examples how students developed their interpretive and inferencing skills by participating in a written dialogue with her. By responding to students' written reactions to the novel they were studying, she was able to individualize discussions about literature and facilitate students' understanding of it. In their second paper in the volume, "A Context for Collaboration: Teachers and Students Writing Together" (Chapter 4), Vanett and Jurich describe how their perceptions of themselves as teachers changed as a result of their writing journal entries along with their students. They came to see their roles as those of facilitators and collaborators in the classroom rather than as evaluators and dispensers of knowledge. By examining student comments about the class, they show that the students perceived them similarly, as facilitators and friends.

The last group of papers presents implications for learning related to classroom journal writing. Joy Kreeft Peyton, in "Dialogue Journal Writing and the Acquisition of English Grammatical Morphology" (Chapter 5), examines the specific morphological changes that occurred in the dialogue journal writing of children learning English as a second language. She shows the progress that these children made in their accurate use of certain English morphemes in writing that does not focus on the acquisition of language form, and argues that dialogue journal writing can provide a context for the development of written self-expression in a language at the same time that oral fluency is developing. In "Personal Journal Writing as a Classroom Genre" (Chapter 6), Tamara Lucas argues that journal writing can increase students' confidence in their writing skills and sharpen their ability to reflect on ideas and experiences. She describes the conventions of a particular type of journal writing and examines the extent to which students followed the conventions presented in a writing class. She reports that students followed the conventions to varying degrees, depending on a variety of influences, such as previous experience with journal writing and perceptions of the functions of writing. John Albertini, in "Coherence in Deaf Students' Writing" (Chapter 7), describes a schema for analyzing the internal organization of dialogue journal writing and shows how two deaf students used cohesive devices successfully in their journals. He suggests that teachers can use students' successful journal entries to make them aware that they are already writing clearly and coherently. This knowledge can empower students as writers in other contexts.

This volume presents seven perspectives on classroom journal writing used in teaching English to nonnative English speakers (see Fulwiler, 1987, for perspectives on the uses of journals in classes for native English-speaking students). Though each author's work has been shaped by his or her own experiences and perceptions, all share a common framework, a belief in promoting authentic and meaningful communication that will increase students' understanding of themselves, the world, and language. Journal writing provides one alternative to the "canned" exercise that classroom writing can become. It challenges teachers to participate with their students in a process of discovery that can enhance learning for all involved.

Tamara Lucas
Donna Jurich

Notes

[1]The term "deaf" is used throughout this volume to refer to both deaf and hard-of-hearing individuals.

[2]A handbook containing a rationale and guidelines for using dialogue journal writing with students learning English, *Dialogue Journal Writing with Nonnative English Speakers*, by Joy Kreeft Peyton and Leslee Reed, is also available from TESOL.

References

Applebee, A. N. (1984). *Contexts for learning to write*. Norwood, NJ: Ablex.

Bowen, J. D., Madsen, H., & Hilferty, A. (1985). *TESOL techniques and procedures*. Cambridge, MA: Newbury House.

Britton, J., Burgess, T., Martin, N., McLeod, A., & Rosen, H. (1975). *The development of writing abilities: 11–18*. London: Macmillan.

Fulwiler, T. (1987). *The journal book*. Portsmouth, NH: Boynton/Cook.

Savignon, S. (1983). *Communicative competence: Theory and classroom practice*. Reading, MA: Addison-Wesley.

Taylor, B.P. (1981). Content and written form: A two-way street. *TESOL Quarterly, 15*, 5–13.

Vygotsky, L. S. (1962). *Thought and language* (E. Hanfmann and G. Vakar, Eds. and Trans.). Cambridge, MA: The MIT Press.

Zamel, V. (1982). Writing: The process of discovering meaning. *TESOL Quarterly, 16*, 195–209.

Zamel, V. (1985). Responding to student writing. *TESOL Quarterly, 19*, 79–101.

Part 1
Journal Writing and the Curriculum

1

The Dialogue Journal: Reconceiving Curriculum and Teaching

BONNIE MEATH-LANG

National Technical Institute for the Deaf
Rochester Institute of Technology

Abstract

In this chapter I examine the role of dialogue journals with deaf students and second-language learners from a curricular and pedagogical perspective. Dialogue journal use is discussed in the context of reconceptualist curriculum theory, with its autobiographical methods, individual focus, and political concerns. Students' concerns and perceptions of their language skills, as voiced in dialogue journals, are explored for their implications in enacting a student-centered, dialogical curriculum. I also examine the teacher-writer's responses in the light of issues raised by reconceptualist curricularists and offer suggestions for use of dialogue journals.

The Dialogue Journal: Reconceiving Curriculum and Teaching

BONNIE MEATH-LANG

The mathematician-philosopher Douglas Hofstadter (1985) discusses *default* words or images, those assumptions held as the result of the conditioning, desensitizing processes of a life-in-the-world. He begins his essay with the riddle or story-problem of the man and his son who are on the way to a baseball game and are in a car-train collision. The father dies instantly and the boy is rushed to the hospital. In the emergency room, the surgeon walks in and gasps, "I cannot operate on that boy—he is my son."

That many educated, sensitive people fail to see the transparency of this riddle attests to the ease with which we fall into our cultural and experiential assumptions and allow them to enclose us. Hofstadter's riddles, terms, and quotations punctuate his concern for our failure to examine the "obvious" and our tendency toward reduction as we describe our world. Gender issues and sexism in language are at the center of this particular puzzle; but one may infer the need for guarding against default assumptions in teaching as well, particularly in the teaching of language to special groups. It is tempting for any English teacher, any teacher of writing, to attempt to forgo process for package, discourse for exercise, writing for discussion. Indeed, faced with 40 essays on a given evening, the desire for a "quick fix," educationally speaking, may even be seductive.

Yet every teacher charged with the teaching of writing knows that he or she is doomed to such frustration. Intuitively, teachers have known for years that to write one must engage in exactly that act, beyond sentence-level targets and computer-assisted strands. However useful these forms of practice are, teachers cannot assume generalization from blank spaces to a larger canvas of words. Students cannot learn to write and teachers cannot learn to teach their students knowledgeably and personally by avoidance. As they encourage their students to write, teachers must write with them if they are also to grow as writers.

In the fields of teaching English to deaf students and to speakers of other languages, this predicament has been mirrored and reflected upon in the discipline of education, particularly in the area of curriculum theory. The 1970s saw a rigorous examination of how teachers come to know their students and fellow teachers through alternative methods of teaching, research, and curriculum development. Indeed, the thrust of this movement, called "the reconceptualization" (Pinar, 1975; Molnar & Zahorik, 1977) in curriculum theory and practice, has been the examination of and reflection on personal, social, and political *experience*. In the process of such examination, default assumptions can be recognized and thus avoided.

Reconceptualist curriculum can be defined as curriculum beginning with the individual in her or his world. That is, the lives and stories of teachers and students are examined through extensive writing and discussion. Reconceptualist educators argue that such experiences heighten consciousness as well as motivation for students. Further, these stories, writings, and discussion can progressively inform and reform educational practice. The tools for such curricular examination have focused consistently on the use of ethnography, critical inquiry, biography, and narrative language, as opposed to more quantitative methods. Educational and social experience is discussed using detailed biographical data and little statistical shorthand. This emphasis demands an attentiveness to individuality, voice, and expression.

Interactive writing, particularly in a dialogue journal (see for example, Kreeft, Shuy, Staton, Reed, & Morroy, 1984; Staton, Shuy, Peyton, & Reed, 1988), is another ideal medium, both for practicing classroom reform through reflection and feedback and for making broader curricular revisions. The dialogue journal has been used, in fact, by reconceptualist educators (Grumet, 1987; Albertini & Meath-Lang, 1986) as a method of evaluation and critical inquiry into curriculum. While dialogue journals are primarily, and appropriately, thought of as a teaching tool to promote fluency and communicative consciousness, they can also be seen as a source for reshaping language curricula. The ongoing nature of the dialogue-relationship between teacher and student and the reflective requirement of writing are powerful challenges to assumptions on both sides of the notebook. The discourse of these journals, moreover, has the potential to become an ever-evolving, reconceived curriculum.

In this chapter I present the fundamental notions of reconceptualist educators and the translation of some of these ideas in the dialogue journals of deaf students and their teacher.

Reconceptualist Thought and Journal Use

The latter half of this century has provided "curriculum makers," to use Macdonald's (1977) term, with a need to examine the language of our students' and our own assumptions, analyzing the deep structure of educational writing (Molnar & Zahorik, 1977). First, those curricularists committed to Dewey's principles reiterated the value of processes as well as outcomes and the possibilities of recasting educational experience by observing and eliciting reflection on processes (Dewey, 1922, 1957). Other theorists, such as Huebner (1975), expressed fear that true interest in students as persons was being replaced by a preoccupation with outcomes and that the emphasis on technical, behavior-oriented language and skills was overshadowing other, less measurable "languages" of the school, such as the ethical and aesthetic.

Macdonald (1975), a curricularist alert to the need for more humane schooling relationships, classified views on curriculum into three categories: control theories (which are outcome oriented), hermeneutic theories (which focus on meaning and are often grounded in theories of other fields), and critical theories (which reflect on practice). Macdonald saw potential problems in all three areas but insisted that the "human intentions embodied in curriculum making," the "micro-macro relationships that bring curriculum work alive," and the focus on *process, situation,* and *relationships* among individuals be of primary importance (1977, p. 11). Pinar (1975) expanded and redirected Macdonald's classification and argued that such concepts pointed toward a commitment to educational thought rooted in *biographical and autobiographical examination.* Following Pinar, several curricular studies have been conducted using personal and dialogue journals or reflective writing (Grumet, 1978; Meath-Lang, Caccamise, & Albertini, 1982) both as data and as an educational, communicative medium in the classroom.

As in the field of second-language education, the work of Freire (1970) has influenced a number of reconceptualist educators. The focus of their inquiry is the impact of society on the individual in schooling and on practice. The personal, argue these curricularists, is political. Society is seen in this framework as the mediating object of discussion, writing, and inquiry, but the communicative aspects of relationships and open dialogue are viewed as integral to the reform espoused by these more political theories.

It is no accident that a review of current curriculum theory is peppered with the words "language," "dialogue," "meaning," "experience," "biography," "process," and "relationships." It is entirely logical that the use of personal journals and dialogue journals has been an ever-present, if sporadic, methodology of curricularists involved in reconceptualization. The dialogue journal is a powerful bridge between life experience and the classroom, because it creates written documentation of both life-school and teacher-student relationships.

It is also entirely consistent that the journal has bridged curriculum theory and classroom practice in its accessibility, requirement of authentic communication, narrative language, and simplicity. And it follows, unfortunately, that the journal, as a vehicle for truthfulness between teacher and student, is sometimes perceived as a threat by certain political watchdog groups committed to the restriction of areas of inquiry and of domains of knowledge in the schools. Teachers using journals must be ever-ethical and sensitive to the fears evoked in the assignment of personal writing. The benefits to curriculum development and classroom conduct are persuasive, however.

The journal, particularly the dialogue journal, places an absolute demand of close reading on the part of the educator and disallows methodological "shortcuts." The use of journals stresses the search for meaning rather than control of the subject matter or student. The dialogue journal's creation of the "dual being" (teacher and student in communication) involves the educator in a constant examination of educational and personal philosophy, rationale for classroom conduct, communication of substance, and, again, assumptions. These characteristics of dialogue journal use described by linguists (Kreeft et al., 1984; Staton, et al., 1988) echo the views presented by reconceptualist educators.

Student and Teacher Writing as Motivation for Change

The dialogue journal exchanges of students and teachers (quoted here with student permission) reveal some of the implicit and explicit assumptions that are central to the educational process and the role of interactive writing in questioning or affirming those assumptions.

The Student in Curricular Control

In this exchange, written in the 5th week of an 11-week remedial writing course for deaf college students, one student discusses her new realization that *she* controls her writing and her learning. I have included my response to complete the dialogue.

01/21/86

Bonnie,

Thanks for your encouragement. I do realize now that my writing is not too bad after all. Infact, I have finally read all of the chapters over the weekend and realized more what a good writing is all about—by telling the truths and facts, and I do this in journal writing. It seems to be easier to do it when writing to a person. Also, I wrote a letter to my long time friend, usually short letters, but she asked me a few questions (interview) about deafness since she's studying about deafness and sign language. I somehow, express all of my feelings toward her questions and I seem to enjoy writing longer letters about me while I was alone for an hour and a half.

I know it's hard to express my feelings to the people I don't know too well. But from what I have read in Macrorie's, I realize that I have to face the people and tell the truths and facts so I can catch their attention. That's another thing I need to learn how to do so I can communicate with them better by telling them who I really am, not what they think who I am. It's more like a proving their to a better opinion or thinking.

Like you've said in class, students have their own control in writing when they choose their own topics—not any other's. Also about circle (Ch. 9), I need to be criticized by others on how they thought or felt about me, my writing, or my ideas of the way I say things or the subject I feel strongly about. Group discussions is another thing for me to learn through too.

I do agree with you that studying in a library to help studying better. I just don't have the nerve to stop there. But I will in someday since I used to work at the library and I do miss it very much. I like the environment and quietness in the library. I've also realized that writing in my room alone do help me think straight as long as I know what I have to say to write them down. Otherwise I wouldn't do anything if I couldn't think of anything to say. So. . . .

I know I have learned a lot lately, it's just this time of the year that I'm willing to learn everything all over again and start from there to the rest of my life, in my daily lives.

In fact, I went through a time of experimenting and never cared about school and life. Now I'm out of, what I would called, a hell world, and focus on myself, my life, school, learn to grow more and learn about anything again from now on—it was before Christmas of this past year when I started to grow up better, and have learned to deal with the cruel realities in life.

That will be all for now. Homeworks to do.

Denise

27 January '86

Dear Denise,

You have given the exact reason many linguists give for the use of journals: Journals are helpful because they give you practice writing for a *known* person (or "audience," some call it). Composition writing is often hard because we are writing for an unknown, "faceless" person or persons. But you have also understood Macrorie's point in the text PERFECTLY. Composition writing gets easier when you use some of the same kinds of facts and realities honestly, as you do in journal writing or in the correspondence that you are doing with your friend.

I am so pleased that you are responding so well to Macrorie's writing. The textbook *is* difficult; but I think it's rewarding to read some of his ideas. He must be quite a man.

The issue of doing critiques in a helping circle, as Chapter 9 suggests, is tricky. I still get nervous when I have to tell people how to improve something. I suspect that you are a sensitive person who gets hurt and does not want to hurt others. I am the same way. But sometimes just asking people questions for better understanding can help them make their writing clearer.

You certainly have gotten yourself together since Christmas. I truly respect you for that; I know it's not easy to concentrate when other problems haunt us . . .

Yes, I know from experience that life is full of cruel realities. Lucky for me—life has also been full of *kind* realities: people and work I love. I wish you the same luck.

Bonnie

Mrs. Mary Denise Patin,[1] a prelingually, profoundly deaf college student,[2] took control of her learning that quarter and developed her own rationale for journal writing. She did so in the context of a remedial program in a class of 16 deaf students, in which time for individual attention was restricted. In such a class, a dialogue journal is a critical tool for individualization. A thoughtful entry such as Ms. Patin's deserves the affirmation and response of dialogue.

We see in her piece a reworking of her own assumptions about writing and about study, a reevaluation of her skills, and an analogy or extension into reflection on learning how best to live. She begins with the reevaluation ("I do realize now that my writing is not too bad after all"). She moves to a generalization, based on her reading of the class text, about what constitutes good writing ("telling the truths and facts") and concludes that she does this in her journal writing. Interestingly, in the same paragraph she mentions, in a comparison of journals to letter writing, her friend's questions about deafness. She expresses the need to be alone to examine her feelings—and, perhaps, her own assumptions—in order to respond well. Ms. Patin further examines her communication in groups, her responses and roles in critiquing situations, and her needs for optimal study and writing.

Her entry demonstrates the possibilities in the dialogue journal for students to reflect on their own learning and to develop their own educational plans. The teacher and the student can then work collaboratively in the subsequent dialogue to affirm these plans and put them into action. The dialogue *writing* that remains as an artifact further validates and documents these goals by recording their development across time.

Ms. Patin's conclusion, and an entry from a classmate the same week, quoted in the next section, raise issues related to another set of traditional assumptions, more pointed toward pedagogy.

Reexamining Teaching Through Dialogue Journals

The use of dialogue journals involves a demand for honesty that is generally not addressed in teacher preparation. Indeed, the disembodiment of the teacher has often been encouraged, making teachers' voices, as they speak to students honestly, distorted and strange to their own ears and eyes. The traditional role of the teacher-machine, with no outside life brought to the classroom, is challenged in journal work. Ms. Kirpatrick's questions in the following interaction disarm and demand at once.

Thursday, January 16, 1986

Dear Bonnie,

How are you during this winter quarter? This quarter has been busy. I have not had much time to sit around and be bored. I always wonder if my life in the future will be like now of what's happening to me. If that's true, how will am I ever going to find much time to take care of more things than I'm going through at this present of time. It scares me a little. I don't know what more to say—all I can say that will I survive real well and will I accomplish my dream one day in my life? I do not want to work, work, worry, going through difficult time through the decisions and marriage, (only if I ever release my picky attitude away and relax—only if I ever happen to meet someone who is fond of me the same way I feel toward him), and piles of responsibilities. Or I can simply climb up the mountain high and turn my life like an eagle—so free. However, I won't reach my dream the way I wanted it to happen, if I avoid the problems like going up the mountain. Can you give me a little of your advise if you ever experienced this while you were young looking into your life ahead. Did your dream every come true, yet? If no, did it come out the way you wished? Mind if I become aware of your dreams?

I'll tell you a couple of my dreams—I want to have a lovely and cherished life along with an excellent husband if I can ever find one. Not only that—I want our love to last till our life ends. Another dream is that I would like to have different life style for awhile—for example, I'd like to work with wildlife animals in Africa, perhaps to stop people killing them and also keep the tribe going without falling apart like the way we did to the Indians in this country centuries ago. I don't want to see them suffering—that's not life was all about. Or I won't mind to work underwater environment like save the animals or work secretly underwater buildings or something related underwater survival. Or I'd love to work on big sailboat for someone like Windjammer or to travel around different countries with good crew. The whole things were just fantasies but it can happen unless ya work had to grab it or happen to be there which is rarely. The problem is that I do not know where to start to succeed my dream. I best get back to my drawing—the break is over. See you today at noon.

Take care,
KimKate

Sunday, January 19, 1986

Dear KimKate,

What a terrific piece of writing here, with, I must say, some provocative questions and dreams.

I am a born dreamer. I guess I have always viewed life as a kind of drama and myself as an actor in this very exciting play ... full of "good guys and bad guys," morals, and beauty. My dreams have reflected that attitude—funny! Or strange ....

My life has turned out to be much better and richer than my dreams. Does that seem peculiar? It's true. First, I have a wonderful marriage—I never thought I would be married, thought I would be a career person in New York City, perhaps an actress or TV announcer. I saw the dark, pressured side of that life, though, and now I am glad I did not choose it. Perhaps my not expecting or wanting marriage made me more open-minded—I never judged men as possible husbands, but as friends and I think that helps. Second, I have beautiful friends, a real gift. I did not experience much friendship in my early life, and my friends are a joy and wonder (and drama) now. Third, I have a job I love—I never dreamed teaching was this much fun (plus I get to "act" a little in class). I also like the other parts of my job, too. I travel a little and meet visitors from all over.

Don't be so hard on yourself. Maybe your "avoiding" problems is really your way of facing them. . . of putting them aside and not letting them control you.

The important thing is keeping an open mind—not being overly upset if a dream doesn't happen exactly as you wished. It may be waiting to happen later, or in another way.

I like your African vision and share your feelings for animals and their rights. Have you seen "Out of Africa" yet? It's a magnificent film—you'll want to get on the plane and go today!

Thank you for sharing these thoughts with me.

Bonnie

Clearly, this kind of exchange takes issue with the assumption that distance is automatically afforded the teacher by virtue of authority. Like my colleague, John Albertini, I have found that the functional progression and expansion of the student's journal writing across time often will include personal material and the expectation, through questioning, of some personal reciprocity on the part of the teacher (Albertini & Meath-Lang, 1986). The teacher unprepared for or uncomfortable with such inquiries probably should limit use of dialogue journals to such areas as reading or content areas, because avoiding personal questions regularly will arrest or restrict the dialogue. Of course, like the student, teachers do control the choice of topic to some degree, and they should, particularly if they suspect manipulation or are experiencing violation of their values. Neutral responses, direct challenge, and change of topic can limit these situations.

Ms. Kirkpatrick also challenges certain assumptions about the purpose of writing. She demonstrates forcefully that she sees the journal as a type of writing that must be imbued with meaning, with content. She does not approach the journal as an exercise. Her other entries that quarter are frequently illustrated (she is an art student), and she and another classmate inquired about the possibility of continuing the dialogue journals beyond the last week of class.

Lest anyone assume that the examination of assumptions results in an immediate clarification process for the teacher, here is a last entry. A young woman sits in my class, a course entitled, ambitiously, "Clear Thinking and Writing." I suspect that she does not buy the notion that such goals may be attained in 10 weeks, but she attends. A shy person, she loathes open participation and reading her writing to classmates, despite their uncommon courtesy. She does write, however, rather along the direction she perceives I wish. Her first journal entry is a study in itself, in its tone of triumph and its eagerness to please:

> When I was born, I couldn't walked, talked and moved around. The reason why was that because I was born Cele- bral Palsy. My whole family were very depressing. They were told I would be retarding and won't be able to move around at all and also should send me to a special hospital and to stay there all my life.
>
> One day, my parent took me to many differents kinds of doctors to find out if this doctor can be able to help me out. They finally found a right doctor that said, "Oh, I can help your daughter to walk, talk and move around" & "She would not become like a retarding person." My whole fam- ily were praying to God that I would be able to walk.
>
> Six years later, I started to learn how to walk, talk, and crawl on the floor. My parents have been working so hard on me. We have moved to _____ from _____ . The reason why we moved to _____ because there was a very good school for me to go. This school is called "Celebral Palsy Center." This school helped me a lot with speech and everything. When I was up to 14 years old, I left from C. P. center to _____ School for the Deaf. All of sudden, I went to a public school. I disliked _____ because it was too easy for me especially I didn't like to sign language. I am oral and always talk all years long. I mean that I always use my speech all the time. I am hard of hearing.
>
> I am very proud of myself especially to my parents and family. They are so happy to have me because they have a friend that their son had the same problem as me but he

is still mentally retarding and sent to a special hospital (home).

I am very proud to have a wonderful wisest parents!! Some of the parents always listen what the doctor said then put their child away. My parents are not that kind of people. They have more warm sweet hearts. I really cherish them very much. Now I am like a normal person.

Innocently, this young woman (who preferred anonymity) has dragged my own default assumption down from the intellectual attic and is forcing me to inspect the baggage for gashes and other signs of mishandling. First, there are my assumptions, after 15 years in special education, about the damage that labeling can do and about how no one, including a labeled person, has the right to reduce other persons to labels in the way that this entry depicts retardation. Yet labels have provided the challenge that this woman and her family have confronted. Second, my assumption about the role of the family must be examined. I am quick to see overinvestment and sacrifices to the point of resentment and exhaustion of relationships in such families. I have often advised parents on their own limits in sacrifice, and I have counseled students on the balance between gratitude and guilt. This family appears not to have had to deal with ambiguous motivation. Or does this daughter know what her family has faced?

I also have serious reservations about the denial of deafness inherent in aspiring to become "hearing-like." I see that there is a basis for some of my concerns here in the student's expressed dislike of sign language (which she nonetheless uses), but I also admire this woman's independence in asserting her communication preference. As a result, my response is rather neutral:

> This is a very powerful piece of writing, S _____ —I'd like a copy of it, if you don't mind.
>
> Your parents sound intelligent and sensitive. You're right. Many people give up when they hear the diagnosis "retarded," although I know many retarded people leading loving, working lives. It is very frightening to parents. Happily, your parents could see through their fear, and you have learned some of their determination.
>
> Interesting—my first contact with deaf people was when I was in high school. I did volunteer work at the Cerebral Palsy Center and I had a group of deaf children. They were fun, *very* independent and mischievous.
>
> I agree with the philosopher Nietschze who said, "That

which does not kill me makes me stronger." In other words, suffering is useful because it helps us grow. Do you agree?

The balance between conversation and control is always difficult. My response here dissatisfies me in all that I am thinking and saying. The dilution, the washing out of ourselves in neutrality and nonjudgment, might be a withholding of ourselves from the other and as potentially denigrating as is refusal to allow the other to express herself or himself. True, the exchange took place early in the quarter and in our writing relationship. But teachers must consistently be on the lookout for the right time in communication and communion to give or not to give. They can only continue to reconceive, to do better the next time, as I hope to do better and better in my communication with this student. The journal will document and evaluate my success or failure.

Teachers struggle to find their voices in these journals as students simultaneously search for theirs. It is appropriate that, in writing, teachers and students journey together. On the way, as I hope these texts demonstrate, both see greater control, complex structuring, and real fluency emerge; all characteristics that some people assume deaf students and nonnative speakers cannot achieve. Therefore, I propose that journal writing, and particularly dialogue journal writing, can be the foundation and enactment of a truly reconceived, student-centered language program—one that requires daring and the questioning of assumptions—as teacher and student continually recreate the curriculum.

Notes

[1]The actual names of the students are used in these passages because the students claim authorship as collaborators in this work.

[2]*Prelingually* deaf students were born deaf or were deafened before spontaneous language acquisition began to take place. *Profoundly* deaf individuals show little or no functional response to speech, unaided.

References

Albertini, J., & Meath-Lang, B. (1986). Analysis of student-teacher exchanges in dialogue journal writing. *Journal of Curriculum Theorizing, 7*(1), 153–201.

Dewey, J. (1922, 1957). *Human nature and conduct.* New York: The Modern Library.

Freire, P. (1970). *Pedagogy of the oppressed* (M. Bergman Ramos, Trans.). New York: Seabury Press.

Grumet, M. (1978). Supervision and situation: A methodology of self-report for teacher education. *Journal of Curriculum Theorizing*, *1*(1), 101–257.

Hofstadter, D. (1985). *Metamagical themas*. New York: Basic Books.

Huebner, D. (1975). Curricular language and classroom meanings. In W. Pinar (Ed.), *Curriculum theorizing: The reconceptualists* (pp. 217–236). Berkeley: McCutchan.

Kreeft, J., Shuy, R. W., Staton, J., Reed, L., & Morroy, R. (1984). *Dialogue writing: Analysis of student-teacher interactive writing in the learning of English as a second language*. Washington, DC: Center for Applied Linguistics. (ERIC Document Reproduction Service No. ED 252 097)

Macdonald, J. (1975). *Curriculum theory as intentional activity*. Paper presented at Curriculum Theory Conference, Charlottesville, VA.

Macdonald, J. (1977). Values bases and issues for curriculum. In A. Molnar & J. Zahorik (Eds.), *Curriculum theory* (pp. 10–21). Washington, DC: Association for Supervision and Curriculum Development.

Meath-Lang, B., Caccamise, F., & Albertini, J. (1982). Deaf students' views of their English language learning. In H. Hoemann & R. Wilbur (Eds.), *Interpersonal communication and deaf people* (pp. 295–329). Washington, DC: Gallaudet College.

Molnar, A., & Zahorik, J. (Eds.). (1977). *Curriculum theory*. Washington, DC: Association for Supervision and Curriculum Development.

Pinar, W. (1975). The analysis of educational experience. In W. Pinar (Ed.), *Curriculum theorizing: The reconceptualists* (pp. 384–395). Berkeley: McCutchan.

Staton, J., Shuy, R. W., Peyton, J. K., & Reed, L. (1988). *Dialogue journal communication: Classroom, linguistic, social and cognitive views*. Norwood, NJ: Ablex.

Part 2
Classroom Approaches to Journal Writing

2

The Missing Link: Connecting Journal Writing to Academic Writing

LAUREN VANETT

English Fluency Program, San Francisco State University

DONNA JURICH

American Language Institute, San Francisco State University

Abstract

Confronted with the dilemma of having some students who fail academic assignments while successfully writing in their journals, we sought an approach to journal writing that would help students transfer the skills they demonstrated in their personal writing to their academic writing. We stopped viewing journal writing as an adjunct assignment and started to view it as an integral part of the syllabus. In this chapter we discuss a rationale for using journal writing, describe the kind of journal writing our students do, and outline the techniques we have used to incorporate journal writing into the curriculum as an instructional tool that leads to academic writing.

The Missing Link: Connecting Journal Writing to Academic Writing

Lauren Vanett

Donna Jurich

Now I am in a foreign country, and few people here know the real cruelty of this incident [the bombing of Hiroshima]. I heard that American people were schocked by the movie "The Day After," and it became very controversial. However, for the Japanese, it was nothing. Hiroshima was more than a million times worse that the movie. The victims were burned so terribly that even family members could not recognize each other. It was a real living hell. On the other hand, many countries have nuclear weapons and try to develop them more and more. Before we think about our own countries, we should think equally about each lives of human beings. Life should go beyond nations and beyond everything. The importance of the life of each person is the basic value.

A Japanese Student

Fortunately, it was the end of the waterskiing season, so we decided to repair the boat for the nexy year. We turned it upside down and from that time on, when I couldn't stand staying inside the house, I ran out to the garage, and worked on the boat, sometimes only pretending that I was working. I always found shelter and quiet in the garage at the side of the boat. I felt secure there. In the boat I discovered a friend, who needed me, because I needed one myself.

A Hungarian Student

These excerpts from the personal journal writing of two adult non-native speakers of English reflect the kind of writing students can do when they are encouraged to write about their experiences. Whenever we have used journal writing in our classes, we have been struck not only by what the students write about but also by how well they put complex ideas and emotions into words. Yet some of the same students appear to ignore or abandon the skills they use in their journal writing when faced with academic assignments. In this chapter we explore how we developed and integrated journal writing techniques and activities into the curriculum to help students recognize their writing abilities, develop additional ones, and transfer the skills they use in personal journal writing to more formal, often academic, writing tasks.

Rationale

We have used personal journal writing for a number of years in different classes with a variety of students because of its benefits for both the student writers and the teachers. First, the use of personal topics as a stimulus for writing means that the students have content for their writing that is easily accessible to them. They can rely on their prior knowledge, the raw material of their lives, as the source of their information rather than having to do outside research or make something up to complete the assignment. Having experiences, beliefs, and opinions readily available as writing topics can be an invaluable asset to writers who tend to get blocked quickly or who have trouble accessing and expressing their ideas in writing (Elbow & Clarke, 1987). A second benefit is that personal topics give considerable autonomy to the students. Though we offer guidelines for the journal writing, students can choose the content they want to develop from the broad range of possibilities provided by their life experience. The freedom to have some creative control over what is written seems inextricably linked to students developing a sense of investment in the writing process (Beach, 1977). We feel it's crucial to begin our courses by helping students establish a rapport with the process so many of them to have come to dread.

The first two benefits have simplified the writing process for our students. The third has helped us as well. Teachers often face the frustrating task of trying to find topics that will motivate the linguistically, culturally, and personally diverse student population that enrolls in a single English as a second language (ESL) writing class. Unlike students who take content courses such as history or literature, ours come to us because they want to learn a craft. To develop that craft, they need content that engages them. Thus good topics are crucial. However, textbooks are often organized by rhetorical patterns, and students are asked to choose a topic to fit the designated pattern. At times the result is boring and artificial writing. Personal journal writing topics, as we have developed and used them, allow students to write about subjects in which they are invested and from which the rhetorical form emerges out of the content.

Yet designing a class using personal journal writing raises a number of issues. The first issue concerns its value in meeting the needs of students. Students come to learn writing skills for a variety of concrete reasons—to enter and function successfully in an academic community like a college, to learn to perform certain job responsibilities such as memorandum writing, or to be able to communicate in writing when oral communication is inappropriate, as when writing a letter of complaint or a report on the job. The question is how personal journal writing can help students achieve these objectives.

Often the greatest barrier students face to becoming successful writers is gaining familiarity and relatively easy access to the whole process of producing ideas on paper. Especially in the beginning of a class, students need writing that does not overwhelm, discourage, or frustrate them. Personal journal writing gives them the opportunity to build their confidence as writers while they develop skills that can be used in other kinds of writing. For example, in their journal entries they summarize information (because it is impossible to tell their whole life history), explain their or another's point of view (to help the reader understand the importance of a story), or write persuasive pieces (as they attempt to convince the reader of the impact of certain experiences on their lives). Thus personal journal writing functions as a way into the writing process and as an opportunity to practice the skills needed for a variety of other writing tasks.

A second issue concerns whether journal writing, because of its personal nature, makes the students less aware of audience and, therefore, more egocentric writers. A way to counter this possibility is to make the writing highly interactive. We respond to students' entries, focusing our comments on what they say by paraphrasing our understanding of their main idea, pointing out sections we feel are very well written, and asking questions about parts that are not as clear. Through our comments, we attempt to make students aware of our concerns as readers. Students also share their entries in groups, enabling them to receive feedback from their classmates. Further, we write journal entries on the assigned topics along with our students. These entries are never discussed or read in class but are distributed to students when they hand in their entries. By writing with the class, we establish a level of engagement with the students; by reading our entries, they gain an understanding of who their audience is and what content is appropriate to share (see Vanett and Jurich, Chapter 4, this volume, for details on this approach).

A final issue is whether nonnative English speakers *want* to write about their own lives. In our experience, students are often eager to write about themselves if they have the opportunity to choose which events to share with others and if they do not feel pressured or threatened by having to reveal private aspects of their lives. By assigning personal topics that are fairly broad in scope, we allow students to decide what content to include in their papers. In addition, our entries, which help set the tone, show the students that writing about their lives does not have to involve the expression of experiences or feelings that they do not want to make public.

Integrating Journal Writing into the Curriculum

We do not see journal writing as simply an adjunct assignment in our classes, an afterthought to more formal writing relegated to odd moments when we have time to fill or want our students to write more. Therefore, we have taken conscious steps to make it an integral part of our syllabus.

First, when designing our syllabus, we identify and select topics that are appropriate to the student population and complement the formal assignments. This process creates a sense of continuity, establishes relationships among topics, and allows students to develop a body of writing they can expand on throughout the semester. With most student populations, we begin with an entry called "Steppingstones" adapted from the work of Progoff (1975). Essentially, this assignment asks the students to list 8 to 12 important moments in their lives—"my first time away from home," "the summer of 1976," "the first time I fell in love," "my grandmother's death" (see Appendix A). This list serves as one source of ideas for students as they complete later journal entries, such as expanding different steppingstones; describing an important person, place, or object; writing a portrait of a younger self; and possibly dialoguing with the younger self from the portrait. We also supply students with additional journal topics such as an unsent letter, the impact of an historical event on the student's life, a description of a stranger, a prediction of tomorrow's events with a narrative of what really happens, and a list of favorite or least favorite tasks and an explanation of one. Selecting journal topics and sequencing them with each other and with the formal assignments is important because it is one way to integrate journal writing into the syllabus.

The relationship between the journal topics chosen and the formal assignments provides the link between these two types of writing.

This link can be made in a variety of ways with different student populations depending on their academic backgrounds and needs. In an intensive writing class for college students, the journal entries function as precursors to other academic assignments. Thus students practice the use of various heuristic devices with highly accessible content before using those same devices with their more challenging academic assignments. When writing an argumentation paper, for example, our students routinely have difficulty arguing from more than one point of view. To help them, they complete a journal entry called "Dialogue with a Person from the Past" before writing the paper. This topic involves looking over earlier entries they have written about people with whom they may have had a conflict or "unfinished business" of any other sort. After choosing someone to "dialogue" with and reviewing the previous entry to establish how they felt at that time, they write both sides of a dialogue, predicting or imagining what they and the other speaker would say. Though difficult, the assignment allows students to rely on familiar content, their own experience, for the raw material.

The following week, students use "dialoguing" to explore and develop the topic of their argumentation paper. This time they have a conversation with someone who disagrees with them about their topic. Though they often struggle with the content because it is unfamiliar, the fact that they have already practiced looking at an issue from two points of view helps them to use dialoguing more effectively to develop their topics and understand the other side of the issue in the academic assignment. The opportunity to "dialogue" about personal topics first results in better argumentation papers.

Writing a research paper is also facilitated by preliminary work in the journals. Our students have routinely used Berke's 20 questions (1976) to develop their thesis and to identify the kinds of information they might want, have, or need. But responding to the 20 questions— which ask students to classify, define, describe, and compare their topics—was always a labor, and they had difficulty seeing that briefly answering these questions would help them narrow their topic and begin their research.

When the journal topics are integrated into the syllabus, the students write an entry called "One Moment in Time" before working with Berke's 20 questions. After each student chooses one moment in the past 24 hours to describe, as a class they generate 15 to 20 questions such as "When was it?" "Where were you?" "What were you doing? wearing? seeing? feeling? tasting?" After copying the questions and writing short answers describing their moment, they write an entry incorporating the answers they consider relevant. They do not find the task difficult because it focuses on their own experience and on a single moment, and they are able to write complete, interesting entries. (See Appendix B for an example of one of these entries.) When they finally approach Berke's questions for their research assignment, they see them as discovery devices, not as hurdles to jump over before actually writing.

The next example of linking journal writing to formal writing is from a nonintensive writing class for adults. In this class, students' journal entries are used to introduce traditional rhetorical patterns such as narration and comparison-contrast. For instance, when students write about a past experience in their journals, they generally use the narrative form. Thus, when they encounter objective reporting tasks in which they have to narrate past events, they already have some understanding of narrative, the value of chronological order, and the need to use transition words or phrases to help keep that order and their ideas clear. In addition, once students have learned how objective reporting utilizes the narrative form, they return to one of their journal entries, rewriting it as if they were reporters giving the facts about a famous person's life. By revising a journal entry into another form of writing, students begin to develop an awareness of how a change in purpose and audience affects their writing.

Through reading and discussing their journal entries in class, students become familiar with traditional rhetorical patterns based on content they have generated about themselves. When they encounter these patterns in the context of formal writing, they grasp the concepts more readily because they have identified these patterns in their journal writing. As a result, the concept of rhetorical patterns now carries meaning and purpose for the students, aiding them not only in their writing but also in their understanding of written English.

In addition to sequencing the journal writing with the formal assignments, we allow class time for discussing each journal assignment and for writing, indicating to the students that we value the journal writing as much as the formal writing assignments. With each journal assignment, we spend up to a half hour on prewriting activities, including discussing the topics, having the students briefly answer lists of questions to establish focus and develop detail, or completing a guided imagery exercise to aid them in recalling the event they are going to explore in writing. In classes with students who do not have time to complete homework assignments because of the demands of their jobs, family, or other responsibilities, both prewriting and writing activities are completed in class. Thus students have the opportunity to write without outside distractions, giving them a sense of accomplishment and closure and giving the teacher a guaranteed product. Full-time students complete entries at home after preparing for the topics and beginning to write in class.

Finally, we integrate journal writing into the syllabus by not assigning it when other written work is due. The number of journal assignments written by the students depends on the number of formal assignments given in a class. Usually, in classes that meet two to five times a week, journal entries are started in class the day the students turn in a formal writing assignment and are due the day the teacher returns the formal writing. This schedule prevents the students from trying to write both their formal papers and the journal entries at the same time and relieves the instructor of reading two sets of papers at once. In classes that meet once a week, the students write three entries at home for each class. From those three entries, they pick one that they want the teacher to read and respond to and hand in a folder containing three completed entries. The teacher records each entry as done, but reads only one, marked "Please Read." This procedure allows the students the maximum opportunity to write but does not overburden the instructor with too many papers to take home.

Activities Developed from Journal Writing

Besides integrating the journal into our syllabus we also base a variety of other classroom activities on journal writing. For example, a "sentence expansion" exercise we have developed helps students tackle the problem of poor sentence development and makes them aware of what makes a good piece of writing work at the syntactic level—a variety of sentence structures, logical organization, and smooth transitions. To begin the exercise, we underline three sentences from a journal entry that we feel could be better developed. Then, in class, we ask the students to add one or two details within one sentence, add two or three sentences to another sentence, and add four to five sentences to another sentence. Therefore, each of the three sentences is expanded differently.

Because the expansions are usually very clear and well developed, we use them to review with the class a variety of specific points about effective written expression. We pick two or three expansions and devise questions to draw the students' attention to ideas that are well expressed in regard to grammar and content. In small groups or pairs, they answer the questions, and then we compare findings as a class. (See Appendix C for an example of this exercise.)

The exercise yields several beneficial results. First, students feel good about their ability to add vivid detail and transitions in their own writing, and they are often impressed with the quality of their classmates' writing. Second, they see that longer expansions, like those in Appendix C, evolve into complete, well-developed paragraphs with beginnings, middles, and ends. Third, in the writing assignments that directly follow this exercise, students begin to mimic one another's styles, experimenting with grammatical structures that they have not used before but are introduced to through the other students' sentence expansion.

In another activity, parts of or whole entries are reprinted with the students' permission for an oral reading by the student or teacher for the whole class. After an oral reading, we ask questions of the other students like "How do you think the writer felt in this piece?" "What are the most vivid details?" "How did it make you feel?" Seeing their ideas in print and reading their own work aloud or hearing it read by someone else gives students a sense of accomplishment and greater confidence in their abilities as writers.

Following Elbow (1973), each student might also read his or her piece of writing aloud twice to small groups of three to four participants. The listeners respond both orally and in writing to two or three questions similar to those mentioned above. After giving and receiving feedback in the reading group, the students revise their entries.

A culminating activity is the publication for the class of a completely revised journal entry by each student. Students choose the entry after reviewing all the entries they have written. Publication gives students a chance to read their entries aloud and listen to and discuss finished products that have moved from a journal entry to a formal piece of writing.

Because students have watched the development of their writing skills, they are pleased to share what they have learned. Often the class breaks into a round of applause or sighs after hearing a particular piece in which the author has not only made his or her ideas clear, but also expressed a triumph or sorrow that the rest of the class can appreciate. We share the students' reactions and the gratification the authors feel when others respond to the humor or sadness of their pieces.

Conclusions

Our perspectives have shifted as we have developed personal journal writing as the basis of our curriculum and linked it to academic writing. In the past we looked at our students' academic writing to find proof that their journal writing paid off. To our dismay, we were usually unable to make any connection between the two. We could not point to strong academic writing and say that the improvements were a result of journal work.

However, after integrating the journal into our syllabus so that it complements rather than competes with formal writing assignments, we realize that the connection lies not in the academic writing but in the journals. Sequencing the journal tasks creates a framework for the use of personal topics in the classroom. Identifying the characteristics of clear, organized, and well-developed writing in the students' journals makes journal writing a bridge to formal assignments. Naming the rhetorical forms students come up with on their own in their journals gives them organizational tools to use in other types of writing. Using journals as the basis for sentence expansion exercises allows us to point out positive uses of detail and complex sentence structures that are student–generated. Publishing excerpts from and entire pieces of revised student writing in class allows us to demonstrate successful texts that grow out of students' life experiences, communicated in their own words. As a result, many students for the first time learn the value and impact of their own voices as writers. We have learned in the process that proof of our students' success as writers is to be found in the work that comes to them most easily—their personal journal writing. Once recognized as valid, it provides the missing link between personal writing and the formal prose required of our students in academic writing classes.

References

Beach, R. (1977). *Writing about ourselves and others*. Urbana, IL: ERIC and National Council for Teachers of English.

Berke, J. (1976). *Twenty questions for the writer, a rhetoric with readings*. New York: Harcourt Brace Jovanovich.

Elbow, P. (1973). *Writing without teachers*. New York: Oxford University Press.

Elbow, P., & Clarke, J. (1987). Desert island discourse: The benefits of ignoring audience. In T. Fulwiler (Ed.), *The journal book* (pp. 19–32). Portsmouth, NH: Boynton/Cook.

Progoff, I. (1975). *At a journal workshop*. New York: Dialogue House.

Appendix A
First Journal Assignment

Steppingstones (Adapted from the work of Ira Progoff, 1975)

You are going to make a list of 8 to 12 significant points in the movement of your life. These points may reflect times of happiness, pain, decision, transition, boredom or anything else as long as they illustrate a moment or period that is memorable to you, regardless of the importance it may or may not have to someone else.

Write only a word or phrase to indicate each steppingstone period.

You are the only one who needs to understand the meaning behind each point, so lengthy or detailed explanations are not necessary.

Your list should begin with your birth and move to the present. If ideas or images should come to you out of chronological order, once your list is completed, go back and renumber them.

You should take no more than 20 minutes, maximum, to make this list! At first, you may find it difficult to think of 12 points, and then suddenly 12 will seem like too few. Don't labor over which 12 to pick. Just write the first 12 that come to you without getting too focused on any particular period.

Appendix B
Student Journal Entry

Yesterday at about eight o'clock I was sitting in front of my table holding a fork and eating tasteless noodles which I usually really like to eat but I lost my taste yesterday because I didn't feel well. I had a headache and a fever. My head seemed to be broken. I sometimes felt cold, sometimes hot. I didn't feel comfortable standing up and I didn't feel comfortable sitting down. I hated everything around me. It seemed to me that I got a great pressure from the atmosphere and I could not breath. I was so sleepy since I had taken some medicine which functioned as an antibiotic.

The room was so quiet. I was there by myself and felt very solitary. This dinner reminded me of my mother. Whenever I was sick in China, my mother always took care of me and cooked rice gruel, which has to cook more than three hours and is very delicious, I think. I would be better very soon under the care of my mother. But yesterday, I had to cook by myself even though I was sick. The more I thought, the less I wanted to eat. Half an hour passed. The noodles were cold, but I was still sitting there and thinking about my mother. Finally, I threw out the noodles and went to bed.

Appendix C
Sentence Expansion Exercise

The following paragraphs are two student responses to the sentence expansion exercise. Their original sentences are italicized. Following each expansion are examples of questions the teachers used to help students focus on how they changed and developed their writing.

1. *At the age of 27, I met a person who affected my life.* He was my boss, who was a very smart and sensitive person. These combinations helped him to understand and to know

the people around him. As a person, I felt insecure and
scared of myself. Also, I was a very closed person who couldn't look at myself in different ways.

Notice how the writer added information about her boss. "He was
my boss, *who was a very smart and sensitive person.*"

Adjective clauses are one way of adding information. Can you find
another adjective clause in this piece?

How many parallel structures did the writer use?

What are they?

> 2. *In addition to this, my sister-in-law liked to scold her chil-*
> *dren, especially at the breakfast table.* Often, she would scold
> them for eating breakfast too slow although it was still too
> early to go to school. More often, she would simply scold
> them for using the bathroom too long because she would
> like her children to come right out after they went in. Some-
> times, she would make a serious face keeping quiet and
> talking to no one. She was not yielding; she scolded them
> in a very serious and sincere voice with her quick facial
> movements as if her children had committed a real crime.
>
> How many specific examples of her sister-in-law's scold-
> ing did the writer add?
>
> What are they?
>
> What word or words did she use to introduce each ex-
> ample?

3

Interactive Teaching of Reading: A Model

MARGARET WALWORTH

Gallaudet University

Abstract

Dialogue journals, in which students and their teachers carry on a written conversation, are particularly helpful as a basis for discussion of class content. The journals provide the teacher with valuable information on the reading strategies individual students use to get meaning from the text and with the opportunity to guide students' progress without correcting overtly. Journals also give students opportunities to articulate ideas about the material they read. In this chapter I discuss some current theories of teaching reading and attempt to relate them to the particular needs of deaf language learners and to the classroom use of dialogue journals with deaf college-age students.

Interactive Teaching of Reading: A Model

MARGARET WALWORTH

The work involved in the process of reading occurs entirely within the head of the reader. Monitoring what is happening in the reader's mind and guiding students toward more effective techniques is not a simple undertaking. Even more complex is gauging what is happening in the minds of readers who lack native skill in the language in which the material is written, either because they have never heard the language spoken owing to profound hearing loss or because it is simply not their first language.

Content-focused dialogue journals, in which students and their teacher carry on a written conversation about what they read, provide valuable information about what each student is doing and how each student can be guided to more effective reading techniques. I use dialogue journals with deaf college preparatory and freshman-level students at Gallaudet University to discuss books they read for class. The majority of these students either were born with a significant hearing loss or lost their hearing before the age of three. The loss thus interfered with their natural acquisition of English. For these students dialogue journal writing, in addition to the advantages cited above, serves as a flow of conversation carried out entirely in the target language: something hard to achieve otherwise because it is impossible to carry on a conversation in the target language orally as can be done with other second-language learners. Examples of some of these dialogues will be shown later in this chapter.

To introduce dialogue journals to the students, I explain that I want to give them more opportunities to discuss their impressions of and questions about what they are reading than would be normally possible within a regular class format. I generally pass out a handout similar to the following:

> Part of the requirement for this course will be to turn in two journal entries per week. These entries should be related in some way to the book being read—they can be thoughts, questions, or any ideas you have about the story. I will respond to each entry and will return the journals to you at the beginning of the next class. Time will be provided at the end of each class to write in your journal. When you have finished, hand it in before leaving the classroom. (If you need more time, you should leave your journal in my office either by the end of the day or at the beginning of the next day.)

Classes range in size from 10 to 14 students and meet three times a week. Students read four or five books during the semester, and journal entries concern all of the books. That the students enjoy participating in these dialogues is evidenced by the high level of their involvement in the process (examples of which will be given later in this chapter) and by their responses to evaluations at the end of the semester, which are generally very positive.

Moffet's (1982) comments about teaching composition can also be applied to teaching reading:

> What really teaches composition—"putting together"—is disorder . . . . Something really significant has to happen inside the writer—mediation by mind. Clarity and objectivity become learning challenges only when content and form are *not* given to the learner but when she must find and forge her own meaning from her inchoate thought . . . . Central is the process that takes the inner voices back into the social world, where the give-and-take of minds and voices can lift each member beyond where she started. (p. 235)

Carrying on a written conversation with the teacher about impressions, questions, or confusions about what they are reading allows students to articulate those inner voices and to receive feedback from the teacher.

Interactive Reading Theories

Many reading specialists today feel that interactive teaching devices, which place the reader in the center, are more effective than simple bottom-up methods that stress word recognition followed by other subskills, or than top-down methods that presume that skill in reading is more a matter of accurate guesswork than a precise process.

In the interactive approach background knowledge, as well as strategies ranging from decoding to metacognitive tactics of consciously monitoring information processing, is considered crucial. Reading becomes a simultaneously top-down and bottom-up process influenced by the text itself and by one's previous knowledge.

Palinscar and Brown (1985) stated that reading comprehension is the product of four major factors: (a) decoding fluency, (b) considerate texts, (c) the compatibility of the reader's knowledge and text content, and (d) the active strategies the reader employs to enhance understanding and retention and to circumvent comprehension failures (p. 118). For prelingually deaf readers (ones who either were born deaf or became deaf before acquiring language), the first category, "decoding fluency," is complicated by the fact that, unlike the normally hearing reader, they have internalized no aurally received "code." "Word recognition" comes from, and is taught primarily through, other channels, which are visual. The "look-say" method was originally developed by the noted deaf educator Thomas Hopkins Gallaudet to teach deaf students how to read because the phonics approach was not applicable for beginning readers who had never heard speech produced.

"Considerate texts" are, generally speaking, "texts that follow a familiar structure and their syntax, style, clarity of presentation and coherence reach an acceptable level" (Palinscar & Brown, 1984, p. 119). For a prelingually deaf reader, this definition is more problematical than for a hearing reader. What, for example, is meant by a "familiar structure"? For normally hearing readers it presumably would be something not far removed from the language in which they communicate every day. For deaf readers, this explanation does not fit as well. What exactly would comprise a "considerate text" in a language in which a person is not able to participate fully? A challenging question!

That is not to say that the prelingually deaf reader may not have achieved considerable fluency in both expressive and receptive English. But even if fluency does exist, it is not a given in the same sense that it is for a normally hearing reader. Hence, the concept of "considerate texts" should be handled cautiously in discussions of prelingually deaf readers.

The third factor in reading comprehension, the need for background knowledge about the text content, also presents special difficulty for prelingually deaf readers because important channels for receiving this knowledge are blocked. Also, because of a different cultural orientation, the deaf reader's world view may differ in unpredictable ways from that of the writer. Background information sufficient for a hearing reader might not be sufficient for the deaf reader.

The fourth factor, "the active strategies the reader employs to enhance understanding and retention and to circumvent comprehension failures," also takes on new dimensions when applied to the deaf reader. Suppose that the text is, insofar as the deaf reader is concerned, only marginally "considerate" or even "inconsiderate" in some respects as a result of complex, unfamiliar structures and vocabulary. Suppose also that many references in the text make no sense to deaf readers at all. What strategies will they employ then?

The concept of schema is integral to all of the above four points. Schemata are "devices by which knowledge is organized into meaningful units" (Quigley & Paul, 1984, p. 108). Incoming data (such as from a written text) are incorporated into existing schemata. According to Quigley and Paul, beginning and poor readers tend to rely too heavily on context and higher mental processes because they lack efficient decoding skills. To add to the problem, more serious deficiencies in their knowledge base can create problems in schema activation. Either no cognitive schema or an inappropriate schema might be activated, leading to problems in inferencing. Supplying material from prior knowledge through inferencing to make explicit material that is implicit in the text requires that the needed information be available in the knowledge base.

Shuy (1985) discussed the role of schema in deaf students' (or any second-language learner's) reading comprehension. According to him, the fewer the clues present in the text, either to the language or to the culture, the more inferencing is necessary to comprehend it. The only strategy available to readers under these circumstances is to figure out what is going on based on *their* world knowledge and on minimal clues in an unfamiliar language system. The views of Quigley and Paul and Shuy provide insight into the particular problems experienced by deaf readers and also suggest an approach that might help them become more effective readers.

Reading Theories and Dialogue Journal Use

Carrying on a written dialogue with the teacher about course content can make that content seem more real to the student. All too often students write about a textbook they are reading in a "test-taking manner"—either as part of a written examination or a required paper, both requiring "correct" interpretations. However, as Moffet (1982) argued

> If practiced as real authoring, not disguised playback, writing *discovers* as much as it communicates. Instead of using writing to test other subjects, we can elevate it to where it

will teach other subjects, for in *making sense,* the writer is *making knowledge.* (p. 237)

Dialogue journals used as described in the introductory section of this chapter are a way of providing Moffet's "mediation by mind." In the journal dialogue, the teacher and the student can together determine more clearly what types of schemata the student is using and then work together to make the schemata more appropriate if necessary. What is at stake here has considerably more weight than coming to a better understanding of a single text. It has to do with learning, as Moffet said, "to work down . . . and expatiate inner voices into the social world" (1982, p. 237).

Helping the Student Work Down

The following excerpts from the journal of a student reading George Orwell's *1984* illustrate how the journal interaction makes it possible to guide students to a better understanding of the text without overtly correcting them.

Alan: When I read 1984. I believe Winston is planning revolution against Inner Party. It was like Orwell's "Animal Farm." Snow Ball is compare as Winston. Napoleon is compared as Julia. The animal overthrow the farmer out. They suceeded the revolution like Russian Revolution on 1917.

Alan shows here that he has some background information about the Russian Revolution and starts out by making a comparison between *1984* and *Animal Farm,* which he has already read. However, his comparison may be taking him in the wrong direction.

Teacher: That's very interesting about comparing Snowball with Winston and Napoleon with Julia. You make me want to read *Animal Farm* again to see if I agree or not! That is a very good idea—to compare things like that. Later, maybe you can think about how Winston and Julia are different from the animals if they are. I will read *Animal Farm* again so we can discuss that.

Although Alan seems to be a bit confused I encourage him to carry the comparison further by trying to find differences between the two books as well as similarities.

Alan: In my opinion that the proles might overthrown the Inner Party someday because Proles are blue collar and very poor. Proles eat the lousy food. It was like the Bolhesviek overthrown the Czars in Russia in 1917. I compared the Inner Party as Czars in Russia in 1917. I compared the Inner Party as Czars because Czars eat great food, can do anything that control on Russia. Proles are compared as Bolheshiek because they are poor and didn't like government. The Czars don't care about the poor as the inner party don't care about the Proles. Do you agree with me?

Alan responds to my encouragement by elaborating, and his confusion becomes more apparent in this entry. He has decided that *1984* and *Animal Farm* are about substantially that same thing: The Inner Party is equated with the Czar in prerevolutionary Russia, and the proles are compared with the revolutionaries. In my response, rather than correcting him overtly, I try to get him to reexamine his position.

> Teacher: . . . If the proles overthrow the government, first it is necessary to make them feel discontented and unhappy with the way things are. Do you see any sign that the proles don't like the government? I know Winston doesn't but what about the Proles?

> Alan: I don't seen any signs of proles don't like the government because they had a hidden mind about the government. The Communist Party seems little like as the Inner Party, because KGB will go to your house for warranty in the house.

Now Alan seems to be shifting his ground somewhat, comparing the Inner Party to the Communist Party—which is nearer to Orwell's intent.

Although Alan has background information about Russian history and the situation in the Soviet Union, he does not seem to be applying it correctly in this particular context. Why not? One hypothesis is that his shaky command of English (both structure and vocabulary) might be causing him to shut out the reading process and simply impose meaning on the book from preconceived ideas rather than trying to puzzle out unfamiliar structures and word meanings. Quigley and Paul's (1984) suggestion that beginning and poor readers try to depend too heavily on inference (guessing from context and background information to avoid having to rely on inadequate decoding skills) could well apply here.

Carrying on a dialogue with this student seems not only to have helped him achieve a better understanding of *1984* but also to have taught him something about a general learning process—how to integrate his background knowledge with the book he was reading. If he had not had the opportunity to articulate his inferences in the journal, faulty though they may have been, it would have been more difficult to show him how to "work down," as Moffet suggests. What took place between us was a type of negotiation—negotiating the meaning of the text.

Bringing Inner Voices Back Into the Social World

The next example concerns the question of schema activation. (To repeat the definition given earlier, schemata are "devices by which knowledge is organized into meaningful units.") The student in question was in my freshman English class. His diagnostic reading test scores were among the lowest for the class. Right after classes started he predicted that he would have a great deal of difficulty with the class because he was such a "lousy reader." The first book was Russell Baker's *Growing Up*—not a very difficult book to understand. After a few journal exchanges, it became apparent that this student's approach was to compare the way things were described in the book with the way he felt they should be. The following entry shows this tendency.

> John: Lucy contacted on Russell too much. Russell seemed that he was spoiled. She gave him a suit and a bike. What about Doris and Audrey? . . . Lucy had treated Russell very well. Furthermore, she should treat Doris well too . . . .

A similar approach appears in the letter he wrote to Baker after completing the book, which was part of a class project.

> Dear Russell,
>   My name is _____ who am now a student at Gallaudet College. I am taking English this semester. I have enjoyed reading the book that you wrote is called "Growing Up." My English teacher wouldn't help me with my grammar because she doesn't want to be like Lucy who helped you writing a story called "Wheat." Do you remember?
>   I have enjoyed one best part when you were at the Navy camp. You didn't know how to swim when you were about twenty years old. That's impossible! Lucky! You got to learned to swim otherwise you'll drown anytime. There is another part I would like to share with you. At nights, when at Navy camp, I think you should have gone out with the

lady who was married because her husband wasn't with her. You'll get some good experiences from her. The funny thing happened is when you kept asking her about her husband. I think you shouldn't do that.

Your mother, Lucy, was one of the other interesting characters but I hate her characters. She was a serious and strict mother when you were young. She tried to nag you to go and knock all the doors selling magazines. I am glad that my mother isn't like her. Phew! You were lucky because you got some advantages from Lucy such as you were chosen to be the man in your family, you got a nice suit and bike. Lucy shouldn't concentrate on you more than Doris because Doris will find out when she is old enough, she'll be very jealous. You were a BIG spoiled boy.

Thank you for letting me sharing my ideas with you.

Growing Up was obviously not too far above this student's grasp. Still, writing about it in this way in the journal and in the letter does seem to have helped him both to recount what he had learned from what he had read and to discuss it. When the class moved on to a harder book, *The Wife of Martin Guerre*, this process of working with the text seemed to break down, as the next journal excerpts show.

John: This part is really confused. I will reread this part tonight to get the right answer. Furthermore I better read careful about the course.

Teacher: I am not sure what you mean, "I had better read careful about the course." Were you confused about page numbers for the reading assignment or requirements? I would really like to know if there is anything you are confused about or would like to discuss with me.

John: As I said that I had better read careful about the course because I didn't completely understand the story.

In addition to expressing confusion, John appears to have changed his approach to a text. Suddenly a "test-taking" approach has replaced previous efforts to apply his own standards to what he has read. Now he is talking only about finding the "right answers." After he read *The Wife of Martin Guerre*, which was quite short, he saw the movie "The Return of Martin Guerre." The next entry was written after he had seen the movie.

John: I think the movie was good. It is much different at the ending in the court. I felt sympathy for Bertrande in the story not in the book because Bertrande wanted to keep the false Martin. In the book, I don't have any strong feelings for Bertrande because she wanted money from him and wanted him to leave. She had no feeling for false Martin.

After seeing the movie, he began to examine the behavior of the characters more critically. He did very well on the subsequent test on the book—perceiving the differences between the characters in the movie and in the book better than many of the other students in the class did. John wrote the following after he received his test paper back: "At first I have told you that I am lousy reader as you may remember. Right now I feel that I am improving since Aug. with two books which helped me analyzing more."

When the class began reading the next book, *Lord of the Flies*, John again expressed a sense of confusion, but this time he was able to articulate its source—that he felt the *author* was making things difficult—instead of focusing on his "lousy reading" and his need to get the "right answers."

John: The story of "Lord of the Flies" is not completed written because when one thing happens it doesn't really tells us what is happening exactly such as: the little boy is missing. But your answer is the little boy is burnt by the fire. Furthermore, when Jack bends down to the ground as a hunter. For answer, I have to use my mind to figure out what will happen like Jack was listening for the animals.

Teacher: You are very right—with this book you have to read more carefully and think hard to understand what the writer means. For example, on page 43, Piggy asks, "Where is the little'un with the birthmark?" Then Piggy says, "He was down there" (meaning down where the fire was). We can *guess* that means that the "little'un" got burnt up in the fire. In the same way, in the third chapter, when Jack is smelling the ground, we can *guess* that he is trying to smell pigs, since we *know* he and his choir boys are supposed to be hunting for food. Reading successfully is putting facts together for yourself—it's good food for the mind!

As he gets farther into the book John integrates what he is reading more and more with his own experience, as the next entry shows.

> John: Ralph often dreams about home. He seems he is being homework. Simon has told him he will be home. Simon prohotizes that Ralph will be back home. He seems that he pitys Ralph. Or maybe Simon is a christian who knows what will happen in the future.
>
> I feel sorry that Ralph did a hard work. He went the mountain first and he had to accept to go to the mountain with Jack so Jack won't think Ralph is sissy. But he did a lot of work than everybody else. If I were there, I would find better way to handle duties, so Ralph won't do all the work or less arguements. Unfortunately, the boys are always curious of things that happened.

The rest of the entries written while John was reading *Lord of the Flies* follow a similar pattern. Although his reading of a book was not on a very high level, he at least found personal meaning in it, which is certainly an important factor in effective reading. Writing about the story in a dialogue journal helped him get beyond the obvious difficulties the text presented and, as Moffet (1982) put it, "the give and take of minds and voices helped lift him beyond where he started" (p. 235).

Conclusion

Interactive theories of reading instruction open up new vistas both for research on reasons for reading successes and failures and, more importantly, for improved classroom practice. In this chapter I have attempted to demonstrate how well content-focused use of dialogue journals fits in with these theories. Dialogue journals focus squarely on the learner; learning proceeds in steps beginning from where the learner happens to be rather than from some preconceived model coming from the outside. Learning occurs through negotiations with the teacher on the meaning (and meanings) contained in the text.

When I started analyzing these journals, I was immediately struck by the difference in the way I responded to individual students. As the teacher, I found myself in the center along with the individuals I was teaching, actively involved in my students' task of making the texts they were reading personally meaningful.

References

Moffet, J. (1982). Writing, inner speech and mediation. *College English*, *44*(3), 231–246.

Palinscar, A. & Brown, A. (1984). Reciprocal teaching of comprehension-fostering and monitoring activities. *Cognition and Instruction*, *1*(2), 117–175.

Quigley, S. & Paul, P. (1984). *Language and deafness*. San Diego, CA: Chapel Hill Press.

Shuy, R. (1985). *A method of dynamic assessment of reading comprehension in dialogue journals* (Gallaudet Research Institute Monograph). Washington, DC: Gallaudet College.

4

A Context for Collaboration: Teachers and Students Writing Together

LAUREN VANETT

English Fluency Program, San Francisco State University

DONNA JURICH

American Language Institute, San Francisco State University

Abstract

In Chapter 2 of this volume, we present a rationale for using journal writing in the English as a second language classroom, focusing on how the decision to use personal writing affected our syllabus and lesson plans. In this chapter we discuss another integral part of the writing classroom—the teacher. As we designed and implemented our personal journal-writing class, our roles as teachers took on a new dimension, that of collaborator. Here we discuss how this extension of our roles affected us and our students.

A Context for Collaboration: Teachers and Students Writing Together

LAUREN VANETT

DONNA JURICH

When we developed a class for adults learning English as a second language (ESL) with personal journal writing as a core activity, we hoped to create a learning environment in which nonnative English speakers previously stymied by the writing process would become more fluent, confident writers in English. Our students were struggling not only with acquiring a skill in a second language but also with overcoming feelings of incompetence and frustration caused by their limited success at expressing their ideas on paper. We believed that one way to help them become and feel more successful was to create an open, non-threatening classroom environment. We thus designed a curriculum that would build on the wealth of knowledge that the students possessed and place us in the role of collaborators with them. In this chapter, we outline the course we developed, examine the effect of our role as collaborators with the students on us and on them, and report on the students' reactions to the new roles.

Personal Journal Writing as the Basis for a Writing Course

Writing for Fluency, the class that we designed and team taught, is offered through the English Fluency Program of San Francisco State University's Extended Education Program. It meets for a total of 30 hours, one evening a week for 10 weeks. Our students include graduate and undergraduate university students, and nonnative English speaking professionals already working in the community or planning to enter the job market.

The course is based on students' personal stories, generated through journal writing. During the semester students reflect on and write about their lives using a series of journal homework assignments that provide a structure for their ideas and help them to focus and develop their topics. The students write three journal entries a week, one required entry and two additional entries from a list of suggested topics (see Appendix A for a sample weekly assignment). We read and comment on the content of only one of the entries, the one they want to share with us. The other two entries, which are recorded as done but not collected, give the students additional writing practice and allow them to write uncensored about personal topics knowing that any private information revealed need not be read. At midsemester the students choose one of their journal entries to revise for publication within the class.

Using the genre of personal journal writing helps students face the task of writing each week with less apprehension. Because writing topics are based on their experiences, they do not have to worry about finding enough information to fill the page, and they are rarely blocked by not knowing what to say. In addition, students develop their confidence as writers as they begin to feel the power of recording the events of their lives on paper. As they manipulate content and grammar to come up with revised, often moving finished pieces, they not only increase their confidence, but also seem to shift their attitudes toward more formal writing. They are usually eager to apply the skills they learn through journal writing to the types of writing that frequently intimidated them in the past.

During the last quarter of the course, the students decide on more formal genres, such as academic essays, business letters, and resumés with cover letters, to work on after their journal revisions are completed. This project gives them the opportunity to practice writing tasks like those they face daily either at school or on the job. During this period the journal writing continues, although required entries now focus on the final, more formal writing project of the semester.

Teachers as Collaborators With Students

An important part of creating a supportive context for writing was that we expanded our traditional roles as teachers by becoming writers along with our students, taking the risk of writing about our lives as we were asking them to do. In addition to responding to their journals, we wrote one journal entry each week based on the same assignments they were doing, distributed our entries to all of the students, and gave them the opportunity to respond to our entries as we did to theirs (an example of a teacher entry is shown in Appendix

B). Our becoming teacher-writers affected all of the relationships in the classroom—those between teachers and students and those between the teachers and the curriculum. The result was a classroom that was not only more open and nonthreatening, but also more democratic.

The traditional relationship between teacher and student is often reduced to that of assignment giver and assignment completer, or evaluator and grade seeker. Writing with our students forced all of us out of these roles as our students came to know us both as teachers who assign and read papers and as writers. By reading our entries, the students gained an understanding of how we approached the assignments, limited a topic, and developed our ideas. And by writing these entries, we found ourselves functioning as writer-learners along with our students, struggling with the same concerns of audience, purpose, and content that they confronted each week. As a result, we all wrote with "real" purpose and meaning, wishing to convey our personal experiences to each other, and making each writing assignment less of an obstacle to overcome and more of an opportunity for communication.

Because we wrote about our lives, the students were able to see us as individuals as well as teachers and as people with strengths and weaknesses outside the writing class, just as we came to see them as complex individuals through their writing. With each entry the students gained new insights into who we were, what we liked, and how we lived. This new knowledge made them more comfortable in class. It also helped them to develop their sense of audience as they wrote each entry with specific readers in mind, readers whose interests and needs they had become aware of because they had read our journals.

Besides affecting our relationship with our students, writing gave us an insider's view of the curriculum we had developed. We experienced first-hand what it was like to complete our assignments and were therefore able to find out for ourselves which ones worked and which didn't. When we wrote our assignments, we occasionally discovered problems inherent in their design. Had we not written, we might easily have attributed the resulting problems in the students' work to their difficulties with writing. Because of this insight we were able to revise the assignments accordingly to achieve our intended goals.

Committing ourselves to writing every week evoked feelings of pressure and fear brought on not only by having a deadline but also by knowing our writing was going to be read by an audience of curious and interested readers. We were better able to understand our students' feelings, not by acting as omniscient, all-knowing teachers but by working along with them as writers and learners.

In addition, our writing served another function—that of establishing an appropriate level of intimacy in the classroom. We wanted our students to understand our definition of "personal" journal writing and to choose to write about events that were meaningful to them but that would not leave them feeling too exposed or revealed. By writing and setting a tone for their work, we avoided being seen or addressed as therapists or counselors, and we avoided becoming involved in our students' lives in ways that we were neither trained for nor prepared to cope with.

We believed that our writing might quietly challenge the students to explore their potential as writers from a new vantage point, one in which they were the authorities on their content if not their grammatical or idiomatic usage. In our writing class the journal became the vehicle and the destination, the process and the product. It was the place in which students and teachers alike revealed frustrations and successes as people and writers.

Teacher Reactions to New Roles

Our decision to write in the classroom emerged from our desire to have both our students and ourselves feel more empowered, involved, and committed to improving writing skills. However, because neither of us had ever before written journal entries read by a whole class, we didn't anticipate how writing and sharing our own work would affect us. The thoughts and feelings expressed below are our reactions at the time to the initial semester of journal writing. Now, after we have taught the class together and separately over several years, our experiences have changed. But at the start, while we both struggled with what we would write about each week, we approached the task quite differently.

Donna

Before I wrote for this class, I had only written when I had to, completing the different kinds of writing tasks that are integral to one's professional and personal life—the required essays, research papers, and reports in college, a few short pieces for newsletters, a number of proposals for presentations and grants, recommendations for teachers I supervised, letters to keep in touch with friends, and my own journal to keep track of myself during the years. Yet after all that writing, I did not feel I had established a voice as a writer. I wasn't comfortable sitting down at the typewriter and recognizing that my piece of writing was going to be read by 20 curious but possibly critical students and Lauren, another possible critic. I was afraid that I would be revealing that I was a poor writer at best.

I was also frightened by the personal nature of the entries. I tended to be a reserved teacher, having been trained to remove myself from the classroom. Somewhere I learned that I should rarely express my opinions in class because students would only use them in their papers hoping to get an "A". But in this class, I knew that what I expressed would be mine and mine only. Students could not use my ideas because they would be writing about their own lives, not mine. However, I had to break several years of tradition by pushing myself to express my own ideas to my students— something outside of my previous teaching experience.

I also felt that Lauren was more comfortable and more open than I was. She seemed more willing to take the risk and more comfortable being herself in class, both through her teaching style and personality. Since we were team teaching, I didn't want the students to think that I was the uptight, conservative teacher. I wanted to sound as open and relaxed as Lauren would. So I prodded myself to sound what I first thought was more like Lauren than myself, using a voice I thought of as more hers than mine to make the initial plunge.

As a result of my fears, though, I could write only under pressure. I routinely did my entries at the typewriter an hour or two before class. Sitting at the typewriter, I would let the words spill out onto the page since I rarely composed my entry in my head. Sometimes, I would have settled on a topic during the week when an event or experience would trigger a memory, and I would think "I'll describe that to the class"; other times, as the typewriter hummed, I would wait for the topic to jump off the assignment sheet.

Because I sat down at the last minute, revision was impossible. I rationalized this by saying that I was only doing what we were asking the students to do—write a first draft, unedited, with concern more for content than for form. I was fairly comfortable with this since it explained spelling errors and jumps in logic. Yet, sometimes, because I composed on the typewriter at the last minute, I would find myself discovering what I really wanted to write about just as I hit the bottom of the page, only 10 minutes till class time. Those entries always seemed unfinished to me, more like statements of my process than statements of myself.

Over time, I found that writing the journal entries was

not as difficult as I initially thought. Once I took the plunge of getting the first line or two on the page, I rarely felt blocked or unable to continue. I think that my keeping a journal and writing to friends made the genre more familiar, and when I thought of my entries as just that—entries to friends not critics, journal writing not great literature—my internal monitor dropped. I found in rereading my entries that I often revealed more about myself than I thought I did even though when writing I felt I was being fairly objective and removed.

Writing the entries for the class gave me the opportunity to explore different writing styles and approaches for an audience that was appreciative and responsive. Sometimes I wrote more descriptively, trying to develop long, fluid sentences, and at other times I wrote in my more usual short, terse prose.

I also realize that writing at the last moment helped me produce my work. The task of writing is still too difficult for me to think about, so the less time I have to think, the less time I have to worry.

Lauren

At first I thought writing journals for our class would be easy. I had published several articles over the past few years and written in a private journal off and on since I was 11, so the thought of writing to my students didn't faze me in the beginning. What I did not anticipate was that writing in a journal for class would be an experience requiring me to create a new voice, different from the professional one I have developed for publications and the personal voice of my own journal.

Thus, in our early classes I struggled terribly, falling back on my teacher voice in my journals as I tried to grasp how much and what part of myself I felt comfortable revealing to my students. To get through this dilemma, I wrote a couple of entries describing my confusion.

The realization that I had to shape a new voice, and actually coming up with one, took me several weeks to do. I was struggling both with my sense of audience—how they'd see me and what I wanted to tell them—and with making the transition from viewing my journals as private pieces of personal writing to personal pieces that I could share. Even though I knew intellectually that journal entries to the class would differ in content from the journals that I had been keeping for myself for years, it took me a while to chisel out a comfortable way of writing about myself for this audience. Not surprisingly, the voice that has evolved for me when I write for class is a combination of my personal and professional self.

My most successful entries, the ones that I felt good about, often came to me as images first—the three trees that played a large part in my childhood or the process of sanding and staining a new bookshelf I'd recently purchased. These were themes that would hit me as I drove in my car or did grocery shopping. Our assignments worked as springboards for my ideas. Once I had a picture of what I wanted to express, the words flowed easily. However, when the pictures didn't come, I'd have to hammer something out and live with the results, like them or not. Up to this point, I had never realized how large a role images played for me in this type of writing.

Another unexpected obstacle to writing for class was how time consuming I let it be at first. I had to acknowledge that while we told the students they were getting first drafts from us, for me this wasn't true. At the time (before I knew the joys of a word processor), I usually wrote in longhand. Inevitably, when I went to type up my entry so it could be copied for the students, I would start revising at the typewriter, a slow and frustrating process for a poor typist and one that went against the rules we had constructed. As a result, when the "pictures didn't come," writing a journal entry would take up to 2 hours! This was very frustrating, especially when I saw Donna whipping out her entries on the typewriter a half hour before class.

Because I was concerned about both the amount of time my writing was taking and the number of drafts my entries went through, I gradually became much more flexible about my process. I would try different approaches, including Donna's of going right for the typewriter, putting limits on my time for writing, or writing under pressure so I'd have no choice but to share those results. In time, I became much more relaxed about the pieces I shared each week.

With each journal assignment I completed, I moved closer to viewing my entries as the works in progress they really were rather than the unfinished products I had been judging them as. This shift in attitude allowed me to look forward to seeing which of my entries would generate a response from the students. Connecting with them through my writing made me feel invested not only as a journal writer in the class, but also as a reader of their work.

By writing journal entries, we became acutely aware of our own very different learning and writing styles along with those of our students. Our increased awareness made us much more tolerant of our students' differences in and difficulties with the writing process and enabled us to encourage a variety of approaches to writing.

After having taught the class over a number of semesters, our experiences have changed. Our familiarity with writing journals has made it easier to decide what we want to write and to express ourselves. Still, journal writing with our students continues to be a rich, revealing, and, on occasion, risky process.

Students' Reactions to the Class

At the end of each semester we elicited student reactions to the class using an anonymous questionnaire that asked students to discuss the content and structure of the class. The students were aware that we would read the questionnaires, and this awareness may have shaped their answers in some way. Yet, in examining the responses over several semesters, we began to discern some common patterns. Because of our interest in our roles as teachers/writer-collaborators, we report here responses to 2 of the 12 questions we asked: "How did you feel about receiving our journal entries?" and "What do you think the teachers' roles have been in the class?" Three kinds of responses to the two questions emerged: discussion of (a) the instructional value of our writing, (b) the student-teacher relationship, and (c) a heightened level of student engagement with writing.

Out of 41 respondents to the questionnaire over the course of three semesters, one-third of the students responded to the two questions by referring to the instructional value of our writing. Some of the students specifically used the words "model," "example," or "sample papers" in their comments, stating, "They have been like models to show the students how to open up and expose themselves to the reader"; and "Thanks for your journals. Your journals are good examples for me to know that I have to specify more details in some area of my journal writing." Some students chose to see our writing as positive models from which they benefited even though we did not identify our journals as such and never used our entries for class discussions. We told the students that, because we were asking them to share their lives with us through writing, we felt we should do the same.

Other students did not use the terms "example," "model," or "sample" but referred to the instructional value of our journals in broader terms: "Receiving your journal entries once a week was very helpful for me because after reading it I was more encouraged to start writing my own journal"; "I appreciate them for your work and those are very helpful for developing our/my writing." One student saw our entries as a guide for the level of intimacy we felt was appropriate: "Your journals helped me to choose the tone of my journals. I mean the openness of your writing." Comments like these were what we hoped our journal writing would elicit from the students when we first conceived of writing journals with the class.

Half of the 41 students made reference to the student-teacher relationship that evolved during the course of the semester. Seventeen used specific terms relating to friendship and family in comments like "It gave a sense of equality and friendship so that I could write more about my feelings. This made my writing easier"; "The teachers roles were similar to the roles of more knowledgable and more experienced friends who wanted to find the best ways to help less experienced friends." Other students expressed a similar idea using terms referring to "closeness." "I really enjoyed to read your journal entries. I can feel like close to you. Usually the distance between the instructors and the students is very wide. Your journal entries help me to write, too"; and "I like them very much. They gave a sense of closeness in relationship between teachers and students because we shared feelings together through writing."

Finally, students described our writing as promoting their engagement with writing and with us. First, they simply enjoyed reading our entries: "I enjoyed reading them. I read them immediately after I got home on Tuesday nights"; "It is one very interesting thing in this class. I can't wait to read those journals, sometimes I start to read them in the bus when I am going home." They also seemed to understand our goal for the class when they wrote: "The teachers roles had been supportive and challenging, they integrated the element (confidence) we needed to write with their corrections that motivated us to improve our errors"; "Their roles have been encouraging students to write without fear." These comments reflect the students' feelings of increased confidence and motivation. We felt gratified by those responses both as teachers who had clearly caught the attention of our students and as writers. The students were letting us know that what we had to say about ourselves had meaning for them.

Conclusions

The four years of writing personal journals with our students have led us to draw a number of conclusions about the process. First, by writing personal journal entries ourselves, we did in fact become collaborators. When we had written for our classes in the past, we produced models or samples for students, often resulting in formulaic, stilted writing. We relinquished meaning in trying to make form our purpose. By writing with the students, we rediscovered both meaning and purpose. As a result, rather than subverting our instructional goals, we were able to accomplish them. By reading our entries and our comments about their entries, students began to understand writing as communication.

Second, by writing autobiographically, we created a context for collaboration, a classroom that became more humanistic and democratic. We could no longer easily categorize ourselves as teachers or students and relate to each other in the prescribed patterns that these roles have historically dictated. Instead, all of us, teachers and students alike, discovered each other as individuals and began to establish new ways of interacting that took into account our varied backgrounds and experiences. Thus personal journal writing fostered an atmosphere that empowered our students and us, resulting in enhanced communication.

Third, by reading our writing, students developed a greater understanding of the importance of audience in their writing. Learning about us through our journal entries helped them shape their own writing because they had a greater understanding of their audience and the boundaries of the assignments.

Finally, by being writers in our classes, we stopped being commentators on and observers of the writing process. We no longer lived vicariously through our students, using them as sources for information about what happens when a writer faces one of our assignments. We increased our awareness of our own writing process, heightened our level of involvement with our students and curriculum, and became more effective teachers of writing as a result.

Reference

Progoff, I. (1975). *At a journal workshop*. New York: Dialogue House.

Appendix A
Second Journal Assignment

Required Entry

Look over your list of Steppingstones (Progoff, 1975). Pick one that you would like to write about. You will probably share your writing with some of your classmates, so pick one that you won't mind talking about with other people. Finally, write about a time when you felt something significant was happening in your life, when you were changing or growing as a person.

Now, write about that time in detail. Use the following questions as *guidelines*. You don't have to answer all of them or respond to them in the order they are asked. Pick the ones that are relevant to you. Write in paragraph form.

1. Where were you?
2. What were you doing?
3. How did you feel about yourself?
4. Where did you live? Describe the situation.
5. How old were you?
6. Who was important to you?
7. What was important to you?
8. What were your values and priorities?
9. What were your plans for the future?
10. What, if any, were your political and religious commitments?
11. Did you belong to any groups or organizations? Which ones?
12. How did you picture yourself? What did you look like? What clothes did you wear?
13. What music did you like to listen to?
14. What food did you like to eat?
15. What were your hobbies or interests?

Suggested Entries: Choose two.

Respond to one or both of our journal entries.

Write a portrait of someone who once played an important role in your life, but whom you no longer have contact with today. The description should focus on how they were when you knew them.

Expand on a steppingstone from another period in your life, answering the same questions that you used to write about the first one.

Using the first draft of your steppingstone, reflect on how you were then and how you are now. Imagine you could meet your younger self today. Write about that meeting.

During the journal readings in class, did you hear something you identified with that you would like to write about? If so, write about your reaction.

NOTE: Any one of the above entries, including the required one, may be handed in at the next class meeting.

**Appendix B
Teacher's Journal Entry**

Today I brought the tall, newly varnished bookcase that I have been finishing in the back room in my study. Its six shelves firmly hold the books, from fiction to psychology, from politics to ESL, that challenge different corners of my mind. I bought this particular pine bookcase because it has adjustable shelves. For years, stacks of oversized books have decorated my floor because they couldn't fit onto the shelves of the small white bookcase a friend had lent me while she was in Cairo. Now, those textbooks and loose leaf binders with years of lesson plans inside them stand tall.

I had never really spent much time with wood before working on this bookcase. After dragging the giant wooden shell up three flights of stairs, I was excited about sanding it down and putting on the first coat of varnish. Because I liked the light color, I had decided to leave the wood in its natural state rather than staining it a darker shade. For a period of three consecutive weekends, I worked on the case, sanding, varnishing and letting it dry, only to repeat these same steps the following week.

In preparing this bookcase for use, I found out a few things about myself and this work. Though I didn't especially like sanding, I loved the smooth feel of the wood when I had finished. Putting on the varnish was different, however. That I loved from the start. Watching the clear liquid change the tone of the wood, bringing out the gentle and varied grains in its surface, absorbed me completely. With each new stroke, the bookcase glistened, its color deepened, and I felt more connected to this process. It was certainly different from reading and responding to a set of student papers, from strategizing about the grant work I am doing, different, in fact, from the kinds of activities I spend so much of my time on. My whole body was involved. I moved as if I were an extension of this transformed tree, my arms now its branches; and for a few rare moments, my mind emptied of all the details, questions, thoughts and plans that constantly seem to confront me. As if in a state of meditation, I felt focused and unhindered. How wonderful it was not to think!

Now, as I sit at my desk and stare at this sturdy structure, I marvel at how the process of preparing it for use was so mentally freeing. And I smile as I consider the thousands of complex thoughts that rest on its shelves.

                                                                                    Lauren

Part 3
Implications for Students' Learning

5

Dialogue Journal Writing and the Acquisition of English Grammatical Morphology

JOY KREEFT PEYTON

Center for Applied Linguistics

Abstract

In this chapter I outline features of dialogue journal writing that make it a promising context for the acquisition of English as a second language (ESL): learners have regular opportunities to interact informally and in private at their level of English proficiency with native speakers of the language, who can adjust their language complexity so it is comprehensible to the learner and model correct English structures and manners of self-expression. The focus then shifts to the acquisition of English grammatical morphology over 10 months' time in the dialogue journal writing of five 6th-grade students, who are at the beginning stages of learning ESL. The study shows that ESL learners can read and write meaningful messages in English long before they have mastered its forms and structures. Their daily writing provides a valuable resource for teachers, enabling them to follow their students' progress in extended writing that is student generated, written for purposes other than evaluation, and relatively unmonitored.

Dialogue Journal Writing and the Acquisition of English Grammatical Morphology

Joy Kreeft Peyton

Since the first studies of dialogue journal writing appeared, considerable interest has developed in their use with various student populations, including native and nonnative English speakers, students learning English as a second language (ESL), and deaf students, whose exposure to spoken English is limited. A major appeal of using dialogue journals with students from other cultures who are learning English is that it gives the teacher a way to communicate individually with students, to learn about their interests and concerns, and to assist them in adjusting to their new language and culture through consistent and supportive interaction. Dialogue journals provide a means for individualizing instruction in classrooms in which students represent various cultural and language backgrounds and various levels of English proficiency, and for communicating with students at their level of proficiency.

Besides these social, cultural, and pedagogical values, dialogue journals give students an opportunity to express themselves freely and openly in written English about topics that interest them. In the dialogue journal, even students at very beginning levels of English proficiency can produce messages on paper, even if in the form of pictures or a few words or sentences, and receive a response. More advanced students can freely write extended text, receive consistent feedback about their ideas, and read text written at their reading level. At the same time, language structures and conventions of written expression are modeled in the teacher's writing.

Dialogue Journals and Language Acquisition

The first dialogue journal studies, of native English speakers (Staton, Shuy, Kreeft, & Reed, 1982, 1988) and students learning English

(Kreeft, Shuy, Staton, Reed, & Morroy, 1984), outlined the features that make dialogue journals a promising context for language acquisition. Essentially, they have many of the characteristics of conversations between adults and children learning a first language and between native speakers and second-language learners in an informal context, i.e., the "set of requirements that should be met by an activity or set of materials aimed at subconscious language acquisition" (Krashen, 1982, pp. 62–76). Krashen (1984) discussed the importance of these conditions in the acquisition of writing, and Staton (1984) and Peyton (1986) applied them to dialogue journal writing:

- The interaction focuses on topics and issues introduced by and of interest to the learner.
- The focus of the interaction is meaning rather than form.
- The language input that the learner receives from reading the teacher's entry is comprehensible, modified roughly to the learner's level of English proficiency, and slightly beyond the learner's productive ability. (See Appendix A for examples of variation in the teacher's language when directed to four different students.)
- The dialogue moves naturally from material that is familiar to the student (for example, past experiences) or shared with the teacher (classroom activities) to the less familiar (new experiences, new ideas, and future plans).
- The language in the journals is not grammatically sequenced according to some preestablished plan; rather, the use of grammatical forms and structures evolves naturally in the process of the interaction.
- Rather than overt correction of student errors, correct grammatical forms and structures can be modeled in the teacher's writing. Genuine requests for clarification can remedy breakdowns of communication resulting from errors in form.
- The continuity of the dialogue provides the opportunity for the student to receive more input on a given topic.
- The interaction occurs in private, in a nonthreatening, supportive context.

The following exchange illustrates the nature of the interaction in one student's journal. These entries come from the 5th month of dialogue journal writing between "Michael," a sixth-grade student from Burma, who had been in the United States for just over a year when this interaction was written, and his teacher. (Student and teacher entries are shown as they were produced, without changes in spelling, capitalization, or punctuation.)

February 9

Michael: Mrs. Reed, you know on this week like the silly week. I don't know what happen on this week. Mrs. Reed, what did you mean about the valentines you said we have to bring valentines. Did we have to made the valentines for people in our classroom? I don't know what are you talking.

Teacher: No, we don't have to send anyone a valentine. It is just a fun thing to do. Sometimes we like someone but we do not tell them. We feel funny telling someone we really like them. Giving a valentine is an easy way of doing it. If you want to give a valentine or fifty valentines it doesn't matter. You do what you want about that.

February 10

Michael: Mrs. Reed I know what is the valentine but I don't know what I have to do and the valentines is we have to give the cards to someone and I have to buy the cards but I can't buy the cards is the problem. I think I'm not going to the sofeball because I did not do nothing about it and Ricardo said I could be the catcher and he break his primise.

Teacher: No problem! Anyone who wants to give valentines can.
If you don't want to give valentines you don't have to.
Talk to Ricardo again! I'm sure he forgot his promise when others on the team began yelling at him.
Did you ever find your pen?

February 11

Michael: I didn't not find my pen. Happy Valentine! I want to give the cards to people but I can't give the cards to people. I give the one card to simon. I think Level 10 hard me. Did you think Level 10 is hard for me? I saw the Thanksgiving Pilgrim in the book. You know, today morning U Chal put cards in every bag except Tony. I know why U Chal put the cards because he put cards into every bag so that he margar him. You said we are going

> to do the art with the shoe box, and you said you
> don't have the shoe box you can't do art.
Teacher: I am not sure what you said. U Chal put cards in
> everyone's sack so they don't *margar* him? What
> word did you put there? Please tell me.
> Yes, we will do the shoebox art. Everyone who
> has shoebox will do it. Have a happy vacation. I
> will see you in five days.

Both Michael and the teacher introduce and develop topics. Because the interaction is written, more than one topic can be introduced in an entry, and topics are continued for a number of turns (the discussion of valentines) or introduced and dropped (the discussion of Ricardo and softball), depending on student and teacher interests. Both people give information and opinions, ask and answer questions, and request explanations and clarification.

Dialogue journal writing, therefore, appears to provide a valuable context for the acquisition of a second language in a written interaction, similar in many ways to spoken interaction. At the same time, the written record that results allows careful examination of the development of students' language ability over time.

The study reported here focuses on one aspect of language development, the acquisition of English grammatical morphology as evidenced in the dialogue journal writing, over 10 months' time, of students at the beginning stages of learning English as a second language. Of course, morphology represents only one small aspect of language acquisition, and many other avenues could be pursued in studies of ESL students' dialogue journal writing over time. However, morphology is a good place to start. The frequent and obligatory occurrence of morphemes in native usage makes quantification and hence investigation of uniformity, variability, and change over time feasible. There already exists a large body of literature on grammatical morphology of learners of English as both a first and second language, primarily in oral language productions, with which to compare results from this study of writing. Finally, studying students' use of English morphemes in this written context yields more insight into overall patterns of morpheme acquisition.

Specifically, this study focuses on: (a) whether there is evidence of language acquisition of beginning ESL learners over time in this free, unmonitored writing; (b) whether gains in language facility can be plotted as information for teachers about the progress of their students; (c) what the acquisition patterns in dialogue journal writing are and how they parallel patterns of acquisition in speech already documented in the language acquisition literature; and (d) whether patterns are particular to individual students or uniform among students.

Previous Studies of Grammatical Morphology

The body of research informing many of the analytical methods used here is the group of "morpheme studies" of the 1970s. Dulay and Burt (1972, 1973, 1974) conducted the first studies of second-language learners, and a plethora of studies followed as researchers sought to discover whether there are universal processes that guide acquisition of English as a second language regardless of native language background. One approach was to determine whether there was a universal and invariant order for the accurate use of morphemes in required contexts among ESL learners from various language and educational backgrounds, at different ages, and in both spoken and written productions. The accurate use of a morpheme was determined by looking at a context in which it is required in native usage and deciding whether or not it is supplied. For example, in the sentence "Yesterday we *go* to the zoo," past tense is required with *go* because the adverb *yesterday* requires past tense on the verb, but it is not supplied. The morphemes were then ranked in relation to each other according to the frequency with which they were supplied in required contexts.

Despite criticism of the methods of data collection and analysis and interpretations of findings in the morpheme studies, nearly all found similar orders among ESL learners when subjects were not in a test-like situation, indicating that there are indeed certain universal processes of second-language acquisition. Based on these findings Krashen (1977) proposed a "natural" or universal order for morpheme acquisition for children and adult second-language learners in free speaking and writing situations, in which the focus is primarily on the message and not on form (see Figure 1). In required contexts, progressive–*ing*, plural, and copula BE are "acquired" or used before the progressive auxiliary BE and articles. The order of morphemes within each box is variable.

Acquisition of Grammatical Morphology in Dialogue Journal Writing

Data

The data for this study of morphological acquisition in the context of student-generated, relatively unmonitored writing come from the dialogue journal writing of a class of sixth-grade ESL learners in Los

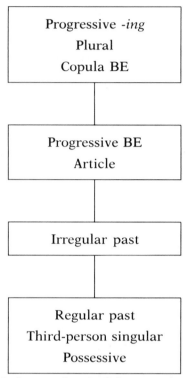

Figure 1.   Krashen's "natural order" for morpheme acquisition.

Angeles, California. Their teacher, Leslee Reed, is the first teacher whose use of dialogue journals with ESL students has been documented (Kreeft et al., 1984). The class consisted of some native English speakers, some students who were born in the United States but spoke a language other than English at home, and a majority of students who came to the United States from other countries some time during their school years—anywhere from 5 years to a few months before entering the class. A regular sixth-grade curriculum was taught, with supplementary ESL classes for new arrivals. Except for math, all subjects were taught by the same teacher. The dialogue journal writing was a supplementary activity done by students during their free time throughout the day. Each morning they received their journal with the teacher's response, written the night before.

From the class of 26 students from 12 different countries and 10 language backgrounds, 5 were chosen for the study, all of whom had been in the United States for less than 1 year (0–8 months) when they began writing in the journals. I was interested in plotting language development in the early stages of English learning and therefore limited the study to those students who met that condition. The students' first languages were Burmese, Italian, and Korean. One student, U Chal, was a bit different from the other four. His first and home language was Korean, but he had moved from Korea to Brazil when he was 5 and spent 7 years in Brazil before coming to the United States. As will be seen, the effects of his Portuguese language background show up in his writing.

One interaction from the journals of four of the students in the 1st week of February is shown in Appendix A (the fifth, Michael's, was shown earlier), displayed from the most to the least proficient in English. There are striking differences in the interactions in terms of topic, style, and language complexity in both of the students' and the teacher's writing. For example, U Chal and the teacher discuss dolphins, which the class was studying in social studies at the time, using relatively complex vocabulary and structure. The teacher responds to Su Kyong's entry, which focuses on more personal topics and is much more difficult to read, using short sentences and simple language and vocabulary.

These texts also provide an idea of some of the morphological errors that occur in the writing (for example, missing past in "when I *touch* the skin," U Chal's entry; missing plural in "My mom come here 3 *day*," Andy's entry; missing article in "I don't want _____ dirty journal," Su Kyong's entry.)

Method

I examined the acquisition of six verb-related and four noun-related morphemes in the journals:

Verb-related morphemes
1. Regular past   He play*ed* in the street.
2. Irregular past   He *saw* the school.
3. Progressive -*ing*   He is play*ing* in the street.
4. Progressive auxiliary BE   He *is* playing in the street.
5. Copula BE   He *is* a good student.
6. Third-person singular,   John like*s* school.
   present tense

Noun-related morphemes
7. Regular plural   They are good student*s*.
8. Possessive -*'s*   We went to Mary*'s* house.
9. Definite article *the*   *The* teacher has *a* book.
10. Indefinite article *a*

These particular morphemes were chosen because, on an initial reading of the journals, they stood out as part of the developing language competence of these students. Initially, most were used sporadically or not at all, but their frequency increased noticeably in the course of the year. One example of the change is the difference in past tense marking in the following two narratives from Michael's journal. In October he rarely marked past tense (once in the entry below); in the May entry all of the verbs referring to past actions are marked for tense. Verbs that should be marked for part tense are in italics.

October 3

Mrs. Reed,
Today I *go* to math class Mrs. G *give* test so I *mest* 3 and 1/2 not *finish* because time *is* up. I mean she *give* the 5. So I *finish* 2 1/2. She *give* the math test *is* easy Mrs. Reed.

May 14

Yesterday I *want* home my mother *told* me to study the Language that you *gave* me to study I *did study* it . . .

Results

I addressed the following questions:

1. Are patterns of morpheme use in the journals similar to patterns found in previous studies of morpheme acquisition?
2. Is there evidence of increased proficiency over time in the use of these morphemes in the dialogue journal writing of beginning ESL students?
3. Are patterns of use similar among students?

Comparison with other studies. To address Question 1, I replicated methods used in previous morpheme studies that looked at use of morphemes in contexts in which they are required. I divided the 10 months of writing into three sample periods—fall, winter, and spring—of 20 interactions each (about 4 weeks' writing for each sample) and analyzed for each sample the presence of the selected morphemes in the contexts that the students themselves had created in their own writing, treating each context "as a kind of test item which the [student] passes by supplying the required morpheme or fails by supplying none . . . ." (Brown, 1973). For each required context for a morpheme I determined whether the morpheme was supplied. The total number of times the morpheme was supplied was divided by the total number of contexts in which it should have been supplied to yield an individual performance score and a group score for each morpheme, expressed as percentages. Results of this analysis are shown in Table 1.

The morphemes were then ranked from highest to lowest frequency of use in required contexts (Table 2). The rank orders were nearly identical in the winter and spring samples (correlation coefficient = 0.98, $p < .001$) and similar among the three samples (correlation coefficient: fall and winter, 0.75; fall and spring, 0.77) resulting in significant rank order correlation (fall and winter, and spring and fall: $p < .05$).

The spring sample, which contains an adequate number of contexts for morpheme occurrence, was compared with four studies of the morpheme production of adult ESL learners—in speech elicited by means of an instrument (the Bilingual Syntax Measure [Bailey, Madden, & Krashen, 1974]); in free speech (Krashen, Houck, Giunchi, Bode, Birnbaum, & Strei, 1977); in compositions written quickly and not edited (Houck, Robertson, & Krashen, 1978); and in the same compositions, edited (Houck et al., 1978)—and with Krashen's "natural order" (treating the morphemes as if they ranked in linear fashion). Table 3 shows the group rank orders and group performance scores in each of the studies.

Rank order correlations between the results in each study and those in this study show that group rank orders are similar (see Table 4).

Thus rank orders for use of selected morphemes, when results from the five students are grouped, are similar among the three sample periods of this study. Rank orders found in this study are similar to those found in others, using both spoken and written data. This analysis shows first that a quantitative study of grammatical features can be conducted on dialogue journal data, even with very beginning ESL learners. Before I began the analysis, it was not clear that the students' writing would allow such determinations. Early in the year student entries were short, handwriting was often difficult to read, and passages were often ambiguous in terms of contexts for morphemes. Later in the year students wrote more, and the writing became much clearer and more amenable to this kind of analysis.

Second, methods of analysis similar to those used in previous studies reveal patterns of morpheme use in dialogue journals similar to those in other relatively unmonitored productions, both spoken and written. That is, students use certain morphemes—progressive auxiliary BE, progressive -ing, and copula BE,—much more frequently where required than they use others, like possessive and third-person singular -s and regular past -ed. This finding gives a rough indication of grammatical patterns that can be expected in the dialogue journal

Table 1. Individual and Group Scores for Use of Nine Morphemes

Morphemes	U Chal Score	U Chal Percent	Laura Score	Laura Percent	Su Kyong Score	Su Kyong Percent	Michael Score	Michael Percent	Andy Score	Andy Percent	Group Score	Group Percent
Fall												
Progressive-ing	1/12	8.3	—	—	12/13	92.3	8/10	80.0	—	—	21/35	60.0
Copula BE	18/18	100.0	18/20	90.0	17/23	73.9	34/36	94.4	44/45	97.8	131/142	92.3
Auxiliary BE	1/12	8.3	—	—	8/13	61.5	6/10	60.0	—	—	15/35	42.9
Articles	59/68	86.8	8/23	34.8	13/20	65.0	43/51	84.3	24/35	68.6	147/197	74.6
Plural	18/28	64.3	10/11	90.9	4/8	50.0	11/17	64.7	19/27	70.4	62/91	68.1
Irregular past	2/10	20.0	—	—	2/12	16.7	13/51	25.4	3/33	9.1	20/106	18.9
Possessive	—	—	—	—	—	—	0/7	0.0	0/5	0.0	0/12	0.0
Third-person singular	0/28	0.0	1/9	11.1	—	—	3/14	21.4	—	—	4/51	7.8
Regular past	2/10	20.0	—	—	0/10	0.0	6/28	21.4	0/10	0.0	8/58	13.8
Winter												
Progressive-ing	17/17	100.0	21/21	100.0	20/20	100.0	26/26	100.0	21/22	95.5	105/106	99.1
Copula BE	21/21	100.0	48/50	96.0	21/26	80.8	59/64	92.2	202/212	95.3	351/373	94.1
Auxiliary BE	16/17	94.1	21/21	100.0	13/20	65.0	24/26	92.3	12/22	54.5	86/106	81.1
Articles	88/95	92.6	57/57	100.0	22/39	56.4	132/144	91.7	21/103	20.4	320/438	73.1
Plural	19/29	65.5	9/14	64.3	6/12	50.0	17/44	38.6	33/71	46.5	84/170	49.4
Irregular Past	27/36	75.0	15/17	88.2	7/18	38.9	24/47	51.1	9/84	10.7	82/202	40.6
Possessive	—	—	—	—	—	—	1/12	8.0	12/21	57.1	13/33	39.4
Third-person singular	2/14	14.3	1/24	4.2	0/6	0.0	1/24	4.2	—	—	4/68	5.9
Regular Past	4/10	40.0	4/10	40.0	0/10	0.0	1/14	7.1	1/20	5.0	10/64	15.6

continued

Table 1. Individual and Group Scores for Use of Nine Morphemes *continued*

Morphemes	U Chal		Laura		Su Kyong		Michael		Andy		Group	
	Score	Percent	Score	Percent	Score	Percent	Score	Percent	Score	Percent	Score	Percent
Spring												
Progressive-ing	11/11	100.0	38/38	100.0	10/10	100.0	31/31	100.0	11/11	100.0	101/101	100.0
Copula BE	26/26	100.0	54/54	100.0	33/35	94.3	89/93	95.7	149/153	97.4	351/361	97.2
Auxiliary BE	11/11	100.0	38/38	100.0	4/10	40.0	26/31	83.9	4/11	36.4	83/101	82.2
Articles	64/65	98.5	49/49	100.0	28/35	80.0	131/172	76.2	33/73	45.2	305/394	77.4
Plural	21/26	80.8	27/38	71.1	4/8	50.0	19/43	44.2	15/27	55.6	86/142	60.6
Irregular past	35/35	100.0	32/34	94.1	8/25	32.0	45/70	64.3	21/90	23.3	141/254	55.5
Possessive	3/6	50.0	2/6	33.3	—	—	0/13	0.0	14/17	82.4	19/42	45.2
Third-person singular	6/20	30.0	3/14	21.4	—	—	1/28	3.6	0/15	0.0	10/77	13.0
Regular past	2/11	18.2	—	—	—	—	3/17	17.6	0/23	0.0	5/51	9.8

Note. Morphemes included are those for which at least five contexts for occurrence were found in individual students' journals.

Table 2. Group Rank Orders for Frequency of Morpheme Use

Fall	Winter	Spring
Copula BE	Progressive -ing	Progressive -ing
Articles	Copula BE	Copula BE
Plural	Auxiliary BE	Auxiliary BE
Progressive -ing	Articles	Articles
Auxiliary BE	Plural	Plural
Irregular past	Irregular past	Irregular past
Regular past	Possessive	Possessive
Third-person singular	Regular past	Third-person singular
Possessive	Third-person singular	Regular past

writing of beginning ESL learners. If the analysis were to stop here, the conclusion might be that these data confirm common processes of language acquisition, regardless of first language background.

However, the methods used so far have provided a general starting point for a more detailed longitudinal analysis in which a great deal of individual variation becomes evident. What follows is a discussion of acquisition patterns in the journals of the individual students over the three sample periods in order to address Questions 2 and 3. Because, as will become clear, the analytical method used greatly affects acquisition patterns that are found, the discussion will focus not only on patterns of change over time in the use of the morphemes, but also on matters of methodology.

Change over time in the use of grammatical morphemes. Figure 2 shows the individual students' use of the four noun-related morphemes, *the*, *a*, plural-*s*, and possessive -'*s*, in required contexts in the three sample periods. [1] Several patterns in the figure are worth noting. Plurals show high frequency of use in comparison with the other morphemes in the fall and then decrease in use for most students, with only U Chal showing improvement over time in the use of plural -*s*. By the end of the year, their use is clearly not mastered by anyone except possibly U Chal.

The use of articles shows a particularly interesting pattern. When articles were treated as a single category to allow comparisons with other morpheme studies, they ranked quite high (see Table 1). However, when they are separated into definite and indefinite categories (see Table 5), they demonstrate very different patterns of use, similar to findings of some previous researchers (Andersen, 1977; Hakuta, 1976; Rosansky, 1976). Definite article *the* is used correctly considerably more frequently than indefinite *a* by all students, except for

Table 3. Morpheme Rank Orders and Performance Scores in Oral and Written Production

Bilingual Syntax Measure–Elicited[a]		Free speech[b]		Uncorrected transcripts[c]		Corrected transcripts[c]		"Natural order"[d]	Dialogue journals	
Morpheme	Score (%)	Morpheme	Score (%)	Morpheme	Score (%)	Morpheme	Score (%)	Morpheme	Morpheme	Score (%)
Copula	84.0	Copula	87	-ing	97	Copula	98	-ing	-ing	100.0
-ing	83.7	-ing	84	Copula	97	-ing	97	Plural	Copula	97.2
Plural	79.0	Plural	71	Irr. past	84	Irr. past	87	Copula	Aux. BE	82.2
Articles	79.0	Articles	69	Aux. BE	82	Aux. BE	86	Aux. BE	Articles	77.4
Aux. BE	69.0	Irr. past	67	Articles	82	Articles	83	Articles	Plural	60.6
Irr. past	54.0	Reg. past	64	Possessive	75	Possessive	80	Irr. past	Irr. past	55.5
3rd person sing.	41.0	Aux. BE	56	Plural	75	Plural	80	Reg. past	Possessive	45.2
		3rd person sing.	36	Reg. past	61	3rd person sing.	76	3rd person sing.	3rd person sing.	13.0
				3rd person sing.	60	Reg. past	61	Possessive	Reg. past	9.8

[a] Bailey, Madden & Krashen, 1974 (reported in Krashen et al., 1977, p. 340)
[b] Krashen, Houck, Giunchi, Bode, Birnbaum & Strei, 1977, p. 340.
[c] Houck, Robertson & Krashen, 1978, p. 337.
[d] Krashen, 1977, p. 149.

Table 4. Spearman rho Correlations of Dialogue Journal Writing with Other Studies of Oral and Written Production

Study	Elicitation method	Rank order correlation
Bailey et al., 1974	Bilingual Syntax Measure	0.82[a]
Krashen et al., 1977	Free speech	0.68[b]
Houck et al., 1978	Uncorrected transcripts	0.89[c]
Houck et al., 1978	Corrected transcripts	0.87[c]
Krashen's "natural order"	—	0.83[c]

[a]$p<.05$, n=7. [b]$p=.06$, n=8. [c]$p<.01$, n=9.

U Chal and Laura in the spring, when they have mastered the use of both. These data seem to confirm observations made by other researchers that patterns of article acquisition reflect transfer from the learner's native language (Andersen, 1977; Hakuta & Cancino, 1977; Rosansky, 1976). Laura and U Chal, whose previous languages (Italian and Portuguese respectively)[2] have articles, supply both *the* and *a* in obligatory contexts very quickly and reach 100% use of both by the end of the year. However, Su Kyong, Andy, and Michael, whose previous languages (Korean and Burmese) have no articles, never reach 90% accuracy. Use of *a* remains far behind use of *the* throughout the year, and Michael's and Andy's scores for use of *a* decrease over time.

Along with learning *to* use the correct article when one is required, some of the students are also learning *not* to use an article where none is required. For Michael, Andy, and Su Kyong, overgeneralization of articles is almost as frequent as their omission, and sentences like the following are found in the journals:

> I have two sisters at *the* Burma.
> You know what happens to *the* some of the people.
> I saw *the* many game.

Like the use of articles in required contexts, the overgeneralization of articles also appears to reflect first-language transfer, with U Chal and Laura consistently using definite and indefinite articles in appropriate contexts and Su Kyong, Michael, and Andy overgeneralizing their use.

Use of possessive -'s also seems to reflect transfer from the students' first languages. Contexts for its occurrence are very few in most of the journals, but the limited data available show that Su Kyong and Andy, the Korean students, supply -'s the most frequently. Korean has a possessive suffix on the possessor noun ("Su Kyong-*e* chek" = "Su

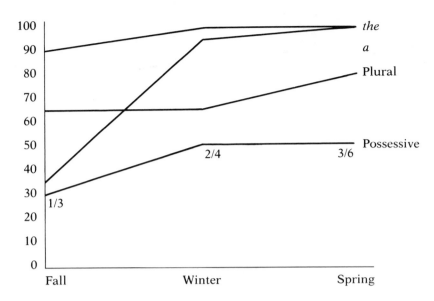

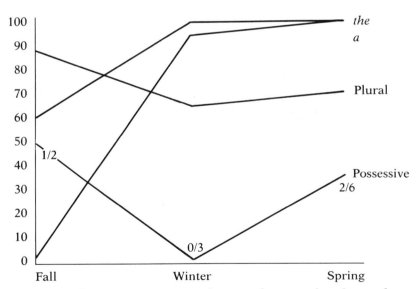

Figure 2. Change over time in the use of noun-related morphemes. *Note.* Percentages for patterns of use of plurals are shown in Table 1; for *the* and *a*, in Table 5. Since instances of possessive –'s are generally so few, results are shown here as fractions.

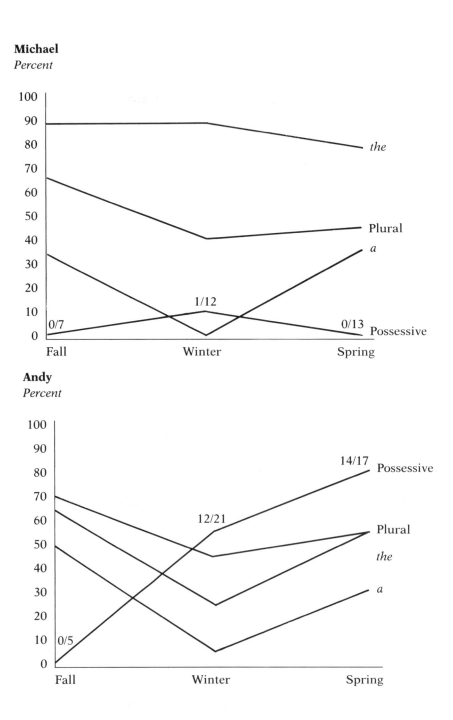

Figure 2. continued

82

Su Kyong
Percent

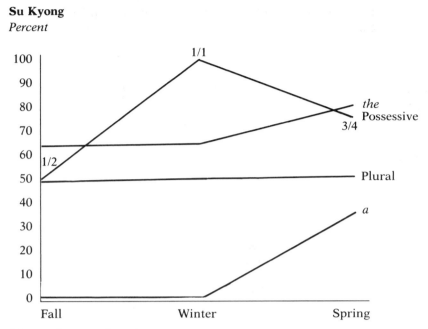

Figure 2. continued

Kyong's book"). Although this suffix is rarely used in casual conversation in Korean, Su Kyong and Andy have picked it up quickly in English. Andy not only uses -'s in obligatory contexts with high frequency, even writing sentences like "Today is one's great great grandfather die day" and "stick to one's own opinion," but he overgeneralizes the form to many other situations, as if applying a rule that whenever two nouns occur together, the first one must have -'s:[3]

> Friday I am lend *Sompob's money*.
> Today in the morning my *kindergarten's sign* is finish.

Even though Michael frequently uses possessive noun phrases, he writes the possessive suffix only once during the entire year. Frequently he uses long possessive noun phrases, either omitting the -'s or using a possessive pronoun:

> . . . my mother big sister son . . .
> . . . my father his brother wife . . .
> . . . my father brought wife her daughter . . .

Burmese has a possessive particle that follows the possessor noun ("Maung Ba *ye* saou" = "Maung Ba's book"). Since this particle constitutes a separate syllable, it may be that Michael fails to notice the

Table 5. Use of Definite and Indefinite Articles in Required Contexts

	Fall		Winter		Spring	
Definite article	Score	Percent	Score	Percent	Score	Percent
U Chal	50/57	87.7	69/75	92.0	51/52	98.1
Laura	6/10	60.0	40/40	100.0	35/35	100.0
Su Kyong	8/12	66.7	21/31	66.7	22/27	81.5
Michael	39/43	90.7	120/130	92.3	102/129	79.1
Andy	14/22	63.6	18/71	25.4	26/48	54.2
TOTAL	117/144	81.3	268/347	77.2	236/291	81.1
Indefinite article						
U Chal	4/11	36.3	17/20	85.0	13/13	100.0
Laura	0/13	0.0	16/17	94.1	14/14	100.0
Su Kyong	0/8	0.0	0/8	0.0	3/8	37.5
Michael	3/8	37.5	0/14	0.0	16/43	37.2
Andy	7/14	50.0	2/32	6.3	7/25	28.0
TOTAL	11/54	20.4	35/91	38.5	53/103	51.5

possessive suffix -'s in English. At the same time, as two of the examples above indicate, he may have transferred the function of ye as a marker of possession to the English possessive pronoun. Therefore, he might write something like, "Maung Ba her (for ye) book" rather than, "Maung Ba's book."

The longitudinal analysis of change over time in the use of the noun-related morphemes reveals no improvement in plural marking. The articles the and a show very different patterns of acquisition, with correct use of a lagging far behind use of the. There are also strong indications that article use and overgeneralization and the use of possessive -'s reflect first-language transfer, a pattern that did not appear in the previous analysis. It seems very clear that, while certain trends can be identified across students, individual variation due to first-language transfer can in no way be discounted.

As for the verb-related morphemes, Figure 3 shows the individual students' use of these morphemes in required contexts in the three sample periods. (The placement of progressive auxiliary BE and -ing together in the figure is explained later.) Here patterns of acquisition among individual students are more uniform. Copula BE is used nearly all of the time throughout the year by all five students,[4] while third-person singular -s and regular past -ed are rarely used by any of them, with little or no improvement over time. All of the journals show an increase over time in the use of irregular past, especially U Chal's and Laura's, who reach over 90% accuracy in the spring. All of the journals except Su Kyong's show an increase in the appropriate use of progressive auxiliary BE and -*ing*.

The students' use of the two morphemes involved in forming the progressive, auxiliary BE and -*ing*, raises some interesting issues. Earlier I followed the methods used in most morpheme studies. All BE + Verb ("She is go") constructions that were ambiguous as to whether or not they were progressive were excluded (Lightbown [1983], for example, "counted as obligatory contexts for -*ing* all obligatory contexts for the progressive, whether or not the auxiliary was supplied" and then "as obligatory contexts for the auxiliary only utterances containing a verb with -*ing* inflection" [p. 226]). The reason for using this method is that it is impossible to tell whether constructions like "she is go" constitute an attempt to form the progressive or simply an overgeneralization of BE.

When this analysis is followed, it appears that in all three sample periods these students used -*ing* to mark the progressive (fall, 60.0%; winter, 99.1%, spring, 100%) more frequently than the auxiliary BE (fall, 42.9%; winter, 81.1%; spring, 82.2%). Taking this approach with the dialogue journal writing, however, also obscures much of the data, which include many BE + Verb constructions such as those shown below. Some (1 and 2) are clearly progressives; others (3 and 4) are clearly not progressives. Most (5 and 6) are ambiguous—they could be progressive, simple present, or past tense constructions.

Progressive

1. and so I told him *I am go now.*
   [. . . I'm going now.]
2. *I'm go to finish* my homework.
   [I'm going to finish . . .]

Progressive not possible

3. Yesterday night is telephone message the my grandmother *is die* that is bad message and sad message.
   [The rest of the context makes it clear that his grandmother has died.]
4. today lunch time *Im no like* lunch but I'm hungry
   [I didn't like the lunch.]

Ambiguous-progressive or simple present/past

5. Sunday raining and Monday is raining but today is not raining but sun *is come* . . .
   [The sun is coming out/came out.]

U Chal

Percent

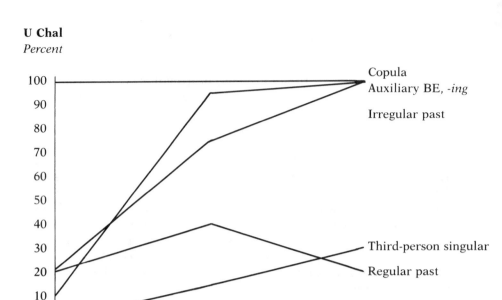

Laura

Percent

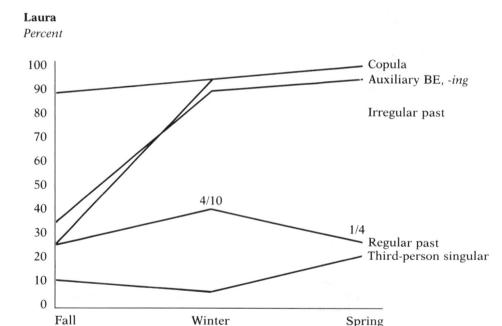

Figure 3. Change over time in the use of verb-related morphemes. *Note.* Percentages on which these patterns are based are shown in Table 1 and (for Auxiliary BE + –*ing*) in Appendix B. Where there are no percentages in Table 1, results are shown here as fractions.

There are no contexts for the use of third singular –*s* in Sukyong's journal in the fall and winter samples.

Michael
Percent

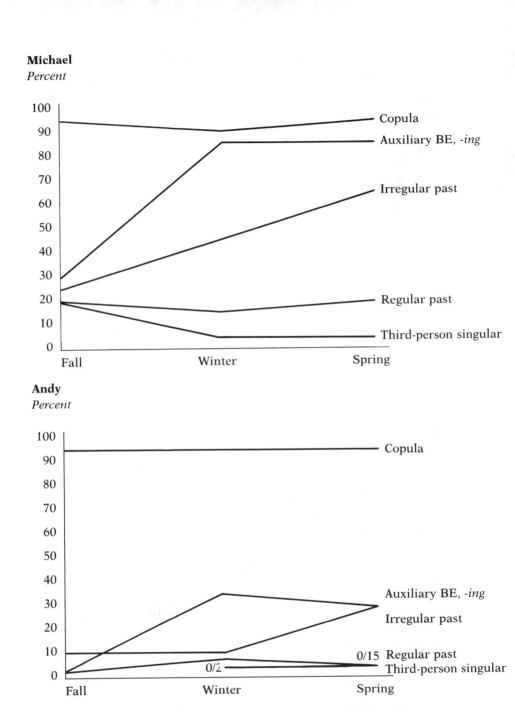

Andy
Percent

Figure 3. continued.

Su Kyong

Percent

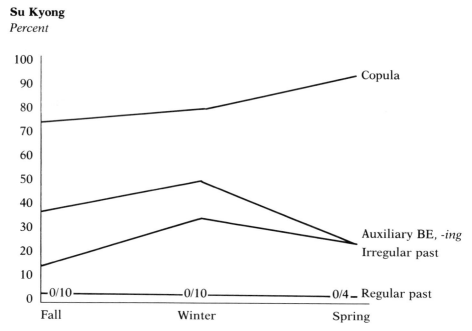

Figure 3. continued

6. I *am get* in a diet because am fatt. Leticia is watching every thing I eat and I hope I can be skinny because is good.
   [I am going on a diet/I am on a diet]

If ambiguous BE + Verb constructions are included in an analysis of progressive formation, a much different pattern emerges. Progressive *-ing* appears far less frequently (35.3%) than auxiliary BE (67.6%) in the fall, and slightly more frequently only in the spring (91.1% and 83.0%, respectively). It appears that at least some of the students are using BE to mark the progressive before they use *-ing*.

Andersen (1977), who found a similar pattern in the written compositions of ESL college students, suggested that it may be more informative to note the occurrence of all of the possible forms used by ESL learners to express the progressive than to treat auxiliary *BE* and *–ing* as separately occurring morphemes. In the dialogue journal data, three verb forms occur in contexts in which the students may be expressing the progressive: Auxiliary + Verb + *–ing* ("I *am going*"), Verb + *–ing* ("I *going*"), and Auxiliary + Verb ("I *am go*," which includes ambiguous Auxiliary + Verb constructions). Rather than using Verb + *–ing* without the auxiliary to express the progressive (16.2% of all progressive constructions in the fall) some students seem instead to use Auxiliary + Verb early in the year (48.5%). As time passes, they learn *not* to use Auxiliary + Verb alone (8.9% of all progressive constructions in the spring) and *to* use Auxiliary + Verb + *–ing* (74.1% in the spring), a process that was obscured earlier. Again, there is variation among students that seems to be due to first-language transfer. Neither Laura nor U Chal, with Romance language backgrounds, ever uses the Auxiliary + Verb construction, while Su Kyong, Andy, and Michael share similar patterns—using Auxiliary + Verb first, with Auxiliary + Verb + *–ing* appearing later.

Conclusions

I have taken two analytical approaches to the study of morpheme acquisition by beginning ESL learners during 10 months' time, as reflected in their dialogue journal writing. In the first, I used methods used in most previous morpheme studies, which are primarily cross-sectional, in order to compare acquisition patterns in dialogue journal data with speech and other written data. I found considerable uniformity in acquisition orders between this study and others, indicating universal patterns of acquisition. In the second, I used a longitudinal approach, to examine patterns of change over time. This more detailed analysis involved looking at overgeneralizations of morphemes as well as their use in required contexts, separating definite and indefinite articles, and looking more closely at patterns of progressive formation. While there were acquisitional trends common among students, the longitudinal approach also uncovered a great deal of individual variation that was obscured in the first approach.

In spite of the admittedly small number of students involved in this study, some conclusions can be drawn from the findings, some predictions made about patterns that might be expected in the dialogue journal writing of other beginning ESL learners, and some implications for classroom practice suggested.

The first set of conclusions and implications has to do with patterns of change over time in the use of grammatical morphology in the journals. The students had very little trouble with the use of BE as a copula even at the beginning of the year and showed rapid mastery. Most of the students made substantial gains in the use of the progressive auxiliary and *-ing* and the past tense marking of irregular verbs, and U Chal and Laura used all of them consistently by the end of the year. At the same time, students made little or no gain in the past tense marking of regular verbs and in the use of plural and third-person singular *-s*. Only Andy showed considerable gain in the use of possessive *-'s*. While U Chal and Laura mastered the use of the articles, the other three students showed little improvement in their use.

Why these gains with some morphemes and not with others? Various reasons have been proposed for morpheme acquisition orders in oral language, including semantic and syntactic complexity (Brown, 1973; deVilliers & deVilliers, 1973), frequency of occurrence in the input to the learner (Larsen-Freeman, 1975, 1976; Long, 1981; Moerk, 1980), and perceptual salience (Hakuta, 1976; Labov, 1969; Slobin, 1971). Hakuta argues that in speech overtly marked forms, in which the inflection takes the form of a new syllable (such as irregular past, progressive -*ing*, prepositions, and articles) are acquired earlier. These forms "penetrate the attention of the learner. If the learner is motivated to make his production match what is heard in the input, these forms are the first to be acquired, because they are salient to the learner" (1976, p. 336). Other forms with nonsyllabic markings, such as possessive, plural and third-person singular -*s*, and regular past, are more difficult to decipher in the input and less likely to be noticed.

The dialogue journal data seem to indicate that in writing, as in speech, morphemes that are *syllabic* (as are copula and progressive *BE* when uncontracted; progressive -*ing;* and irregular past, as in "He *went*") tend to be acquired more quickly and therefore may be more salient to the learner. Perceptual salience is a slippery concept and is not always tied to syllabicity. Copula and progressive *BE* are often contracted and therefore not always syllabic. Andy quickly picked up on the use of possessive –'*s*, which is not syllabic. However, syllabicity does seem to play a role here.

When rules for the use of syllabic morphemes are easily learned (which is the case for copula and the progressive morphemes) or require the learning of a new word (as with irregular past verbs), such morphemes may be acquired in a naturalistic, communicative context.[5] When rules for syllabic morphemes are difficult to learn (which is the case for articles), naturalistic acquisition, or at least use of the morphemes in naturalistic communication, does not seem to occur as quickly. Laura and U Chal did master article use, but they could transfer rules for article use in Italian and Portuguese to English. The other students had more trouble with articles.

Morphemes that tend not to be syllabic (plural, in "two girl*s*"; possessive in "John'*s* shoes"; regular past, in "she seem*ed* smart") are acquired more slowly. Possibly, beginning ESL learners simply will not use these morphemes in communicative, relatively unmonitored writing contexts even though rules for their use are easily taught and learned and have been taught and drilled extensively in class (as they had been in this class). Getting students to use articles and nonsyllabic morphemes correctly in their writing may require teaching them methods for carefully editing pieces they have written.[6]

Second, while some overall trends are common across students, there is also considerable individual variation in their acquisition processes, which seems to be a result of first-language transfer. Therefore, as Gass and Selinker (1983) argue,

> [I]t is indeed possible and not incompatible to view second language acquisition as both (1) a process of hypothesis testing in which learners create knowledge from the second language data they have available to them while *at the same time* viewing it as (2) a process of utilizing first language knowledge as well as knowledge of other languages known to the learners in the creation of a learner language. (p. 7)

Language universals and natural orders of morpheme acquisition notwithstanding, the search for and belief in universal processes should not blind teachers and researchers to the richness of individual variation that is also present, to the extent that they develop inappropriate and self-defeating expectations of students. It will simply frustrate teachers and do the students a great disservice to expect them all to perform alike.

Third, dialogue journal writing does reflect changes in students' language proficiency over time, even at the earliest stages of second language acquisition. I was able to quantify and plot this growth for each student, including the least proficient in English.

Clearly, dialogue journal writing can serve as a valuable resource for teachers, enabling them to follow their students' progress in extended writing that is student-generated, written for purposes other than evaluation, and relatively unmonitored. From reading student entries, teachers can discover a great deal not only about their students as human beings, but also about what they are learning, where they might be having trouble, and where future lessons might focus. Although I have looked only at the acquisition of morphology in this study, the writing yields a wealth of information about each student's progress, from the smallest features of the language to discourse and interaction patterns.

Finally, the various examples of text shown throughout the chapter demonstrate that ESL learners can compose and express themselves in written English long before they have mastered its forms and structures. Even at the beginning of the year, when morphology was at the earliest stages of development, these students were writing and reading meaningful texts in their journals. As the year progressed they wrote narratives, described events and problems, and even argued their points of view. In the meantime, the forms and structures of written English continued to develop.

References

Andersen, R.W. (1977). The impoverished state of cross-sectional acquisition/accuracy methodology. In L.A. Henning (Ed.), *Proceedings of the Los Angeles Second Language Acquisition Research Forum.* Los Angeles, CA: UCLA. (ERIC Document Reproduction Service No. ED 146 780)

Bailey, N., Madden, C., & Krashen, S. D. (1974). Is there a "natural sequence" in adult second language learning? *Language Learning, 24*(2), 235–243.

Brown, R. (1973). *A first language: The early stages.* Cambridge, MA: Harvard University Press.

DeVilliers, J.G., & deVilliers, P. A. (1973). A cross-sectional study of the acquisition of grammatical morphemes in child speech. *Journal of Psycholinguistic Research, 2,* 267–278.

Dulay, H. C., & Burt, M. K. (1972). Goofing: An indicator of children's second language learning strategies. *Language Learning, 22*(2), 235–252.

Dulay, H.C., & Burt, M.K. (1973). Should we teach children syntax? *Language Learning,23*(2), 245–258.

Dulay, H.C., & Burt, M. K. (1974). Natural sequences in child second language acquisition. *Language Learning, 24*(1), 37–53.

Gass, S., & Selinker, L. (1983). Introduction. In S. Gass & L. Selinker (Eds.), *Language transfer in language learning* (pp. 1–18). Rowley, MA: Newbury House.

Hakuta, K. (1976). Becoming bilingual: A case study of a Japanese child learning English as a second language. *Language Learning, 26*(2), 321–351.

Hakuta, K., & Cancino, H. (1977). Trends in second language acquisition research. *Harvard Educational Review, 47*(3), 294–316.

Houck, N., Robertson, J., & Krashen, S. D. (1978). On the domain of the conscious grammar: Morpheme orders for corrected and uncorrected ESL student transcriptions. *TESOL Quarterly, 12,* 335–339.

Krashen, S. D. (1977). Some issues relating to the monitor model. In H.D. Brown, C. Yorio, & R. Crymes (Eds.), *Teaching and learning English as a second language: Trends in research and practice* (pp. 144–158). Washington, DC: TESOL.

Krashen, S. D. (1982). *Principles and practice in second language acquisition.* Oxford, England: Pergamon Press.

Krashen, S. D. (1984). *Writing: Research, theory and applications.* Oxford, England: Pergamon Press.

Krashen, S. D., Houck, N., Giunchi, P., Bode, S., Birnbaum, R., &

Strei, G. (1977). Difficulty order for grammatical morphemes for adult second language performers using free speech. *TESOL Quarterly, 11*, 338–241.

Kreeft, J. (1984). *Dialogue journal writing and the acquisition of grammatical morphology in English as a second language.* Doctoral dissertation, Georgetown University, Washington, DC.

Kreeft, J., Shuy, R. W., Staton, J., Reed, L., & Morroy, R. (1984). *Dialogue writing: Analysis of student-teacher interactive writing in the learning of English as a second language* (Report No. NIE-G–83–0030). Washington, DC: Center for Applied Linguistics.

Labov, W. (1969). Contraction, deletion, and the inherent variability of the English copula. *Language, 45*, 715–762.

Larsen-Freeman, D. (1975). The acquisition of grammatical morphemes by adult ESL students. *TESOL Quarterly, 9*, 409–419.

Larsen-Freeman, D. (1976). An explanation of the morpheme acquisition order of second language learners. *Language Learning, 26*(1), 125–134.

Lightbown, P. M. (1983). Exploring relationships between developmental and instructional sequences in L2 acquisition. In H. W. Seliger & M. H. Long (Eds.), *Classroom oriented research in second language acquisition* (pp. 217–243). Rowley, MA: Newbury House.

Long, M. H. (1981). Questions for foreigner talk discourse. *Language Learning, 31*(1), 135–157.

Moerk, E. L. (1980). Relationships between parental input frequencies and children's language acquisition: A reanalysis of Brown's data. *Journal of Child Language, 7*(1), 105–118.

Peyton, J. K. (1986). Literacy through written interaction. *Passage: A Journal of Refugee Education, 2*(1), 24–29.

Pica, T. (1982). *Second language acquisition in different language contexts* Doctoral dissertation, University of Pennsylvania, Philadelphia, PA.

Pica, T. (1983). Adult acquisition of English as a second language under different conditions of exposure. *Language Learning, 33*(4), 465–497.

Pica, T. (1984). L1 transfer and L2 complexity as factors in syllabus design. *TESOL Quarterly, 18*, 698–704.

Rosansky, E. J. (1976). *Second language acquisition research: A question of methods.* Doctoral dissertation, Harvard University, Cambridge, MA.

Slobin, D. I. (1971). Developmental psycholinguistics. In W. O. Dingwall (Ed.), *A survey of linguistic science* (pp. 279–410). College Park, MD: University of Maryland.

Staton, J. 1984. Dialogue journals as a means of enabling written language acquisition. In J. Kreeft, R. W. Shuy, J. Staton, L. Reed, & R. Morroy, *Dialogue writing: Analysis of student-teacher interactive writing in the learning of English as a second language* (Report No. NIE-G–83–0030). Washington, DC: Center for Applied Linguistics.

Staton, J., Shuy, R. W., Kreeft, J., & Reed, L. (1982). *Analysis of dialogue journal writing as a communicative event* (Report No. NIE-G–80–0122). Washington, DC: Center for Applied Linguistics.

Staton, J., Shuy, R. W., Peyton, J. K., & Reed, L. (1988). *Dialogue journal communications: Classroom, linguistic, social and cognitive views.* Norwood, NJ: Ablex.

Author's Note

The research for this study was conducted with the support of the National Institute of Education, NIE-G–83–0030. I am grateful to the National Institute of Education, the Office of Educational Research and Improvement, and the Center for Language Education and Research for continuing support of research on dialogue journal writing. I am also grateful to Ralph Fasold for performing the statistical analyses and to Ralph Fasold, Roger W. Shuy, Jana Staton, and Walt Wolfram for useful comments on earlier versions of this chapter.

Notes

[1] In this part of the study all morphemes are included whether or not there are five contexts for their occurrence.

[2] It is important to emphasize *previous* rather than *first* language when speaking of U Chal because his first language is Korean and his second language, Portuguese.

[3] Hakuta (1976) found a pattern for possessive marking in the speech of his Japanese subject, Uguisu, similar to the one I found in Andy's journal. While Uguisu marked plurals very infrequently, she reached 90% accuracy with the use of possessive -'s and overgeneralized the form to possessive pronouns (*he's*, *they's*) as well. Hakuta suggests that this could be a result of Japanese influence—in Japanese a postposed article *no* appears in the same position as the -'s in English.

[4] There are also many instances of overgeneralizations of *BE* to inappropriate contexts. Overgeneralizations of all of the morphemes in this study are discussed in Kreeft, 1984.

[5] Pica (1982, 1983) found that explicit instruction in the use of progressive

-ing, an easily learned rule, resulted in students' not only using it consistently in required contexts, but also overgeneralizing it to contexts in which it was not required.

[6]There is evidence (cf. Pica, 1984) that direct instruction does accelerate the accurate use of easy-to-learn morphemes such as third-person singular *-s*. Pica does not, however, specify the conditions under which they are produced. What we have seen in these data is that this knowledge, if in fact these particular students display it in other writing, has not yet been transferred to their dialogue journal writing.

Appendix A
Examples of Dialogue Journal Interactions

U Chal: . . . I know and I read that scientist was stunding about dolphins language. Last year when I was in Brazil I was in the beach and I saw a dophin dead on the sand and when I touch the skin is like sofet and then when I eat the lunch and I go to see the dolphin some birds was eating the dolphin.

Teacher: The dolphins have even been trained to do undersea work for the Navy. They seem to have an intelligence. The birds help to clean the beach by eating the dead animals. The dolphin's skin has no scales—we expect an animal that looks like a fish to have scales.

Andy: Today I am happy, because give me "New Journal". I like "New Journal". I in picture name is "Korea bird and Korea dragon and sun". I am happy. My mom come here 3 day. I am happy. My mom give me present. "Make toy". "Stamps" Korea book (cartoon) and other is give to me. I am happy happy. "Faster come here mom please." Today I am second came to school. "Oh, No". O.K. Tomorrow I am first. "No more". only I am $happy^1$ + $happy^2$ $happy^3$ = $happy^9$. See you tomorrow. bye

Teacher: Your Mother will be happy to see you! You can tell your Mother you are learning to speak and to write more English every day. You were at school before I was today. Thursday we will go back outside before school because Mrs. Reed has to go out to watch all of the students.

We learned about the cold Arctic Biome. Would you like to live there?

Laura: Dear mrs Reed I like the red hart is ruely nice I hope yaw like my. the fish was very good. Mrs. G- sad I am going to 6 lavel I am ruealy happy. Simon go to. I wish yaw a very happy Valentine to yaw and your asmont.

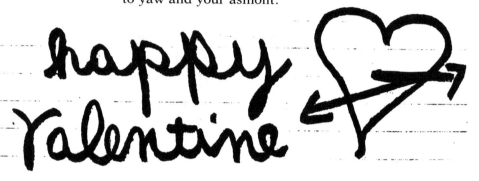

Teacher: I love your valentine. It is so beautiful. The red name and the red heart are so pretty. I like it so much because you made it for me! Thank you. It is one of my favorite valentines. I hope your weekend is fun and you come back on Tuesday ready to go to level 6!

Su Kyong: today I looke the jernol is doly if I do the now jernol and if this jernol is doly my har is not clyn if I do the my now jernol I don't wont doly jernol and today moning sandra is mad me oumus shes borsday I have to got the pljons is her borsday

Teacher: Can you make a big, big birthday card for Sandra's birthday? She would like that.
I see your word study list in your journal. I am happy you are studying it.
If you keep writing you will get a new journal.

Appendix B. Use of Auxiliary and -ing to Form the Progressive

	Fall		Winter		Spring	
	Score	Percent	Score	Percent	Score	Percent
U Chal	1/13	7.7	16/17	94.1	11/11	100.0
Laura	1/4	25.0	21/22	95.5	38/39	97.4
Michael	4/14	28.6	24/28	85.7	26/32	81.3
Andy	0/18	0.0	11/37	29.7	4/17	23.5
Su Kyong	7/19	36.8	13/26	50.0	4/13	30.8
TOTAL	13/68	19.1	85/130	65.4	83/112	74.1

6

Personal Journal Writing as a Classroom Genre

TAMARA LUCAS

Southwest Center for Educational Equity
ARC Associates
Oakland, CA

Abstract

Journal writing, used in different ways and for different purposes, is now a part of many English as a second language (ESL) classrooms. Practitioners and researchers alike have argued that ESL students benefit in a variety of ways from writing journals. In this chapter I examine the journal writing assigned in an adult ESL writing course: the conventions of the writing, including those presented by the teachers both implicitly and explicitly, and the ways in which nine case study students responded to this type of writing. Their individual responses to the personal, reflective nature of the writing were influenced by such factors as previous writing experiences, life experiences, and cultural and personal values regarding written reflection on personal experiences. As a result of their engagement with the writing, students reported increased confidence in their ability to write in English, renewed or newfound commitment to improving their skills, and a deepened understanding of themselves.

Personal Journal Writing as a Classroom Genre

TAMARA LUCAS

The nature of the writing process and the interaction between writers and their readers that is involved in writing make it a medium through which writers can learn and make meaning for themselves (Applebee, 1981, 1984; Britton, 1970; Bruner, 1966; Langer & Applebee, 1986; Vygotsky, 1962). In classrooms, students' writing provides the opportunity for constructive interaction with and feedback from the teacher and for the conscious, internal structuring of meaning that is part of the writing process (Applebee, 1981, 1984; Applebee & Langer, 1983; Britton, Burgess, Martin, McLeod, & Rosen, 1975; Vygotsky, 1962). When students write about themselves, they have the additional benefit of interacting about and structuring meaning around content that they know about and in which they are personally invested.

Some teachers use journals in their classes in the hope that their students will realize these benefits and that their language and writing skills will develop as well as their understanding of ideas, themselves, and the world. Such teachers have reported a variety of positive results from using journal writing in the classroom, including the establishment of rapport between students and teachers (Peyton, 1988), "cognitive demands" placed on students "to elaborate his or her own thinking" (Staton, 1988, p. 317), the development of "a foundation of 'mutuality' or shared understanding" (Staton, 1988, p. 313), and the development of language skills (Peyton, this volume).

However, classroom journals come in many different guises. For example, the dialogue journals examined in the research mentioned above (see also Albertini, Meath-Lang, and Walworth, this volume) are different in some fundamental ways from the type of journal writing described in this chapter in terms of number, length, and frequency of journal entries; typical content; and relationship to other class activities. Some classroom journals focus only on course content, others only on the students' experiences, and still others on whatever the students choose to write about. Before examining the effects or benefits of any classroom journal writing, the characteristics of the type of journal writing involved, i.e., the conventions of the genre, must first be determined.

I focus here on one type of classroom journal writing, the personal journal, reporting on a study of the use of personal journals in an adult English as a second language (ESL) class. I show that this type of writing constitutes a genre with a set of conventions and functions and particular effects on students. I argue first that in teaching writing, instructors teach a genre with a set of features of form, content, use, and audience; second, that different students respond in different ways to being asked to engage in a particular genre; and third, that engagement with classroom personal journal writing can have positive effects on students' engagement with other genres, such as academic essays.

I consider the personal journal writing examined in this study to be a *genre*, following Ferguson's definition of genre as "a unit of discourse conventionalized in a given community at a certain time, having an internal sequential structure and a set of features of form, content, and use that distinguish it from others in the repertoire of the community" (1986, p. 208). To Ferguson's "features of form, content, and use," I add *audience*. However, though genres do have characteristic features, the nature of genre is such that "very few necessary elements exist" for any particular one. Boundaries between genres are "indistinct and shifting, overlapping and allowing intricate mixture" (Fowler, 1982, p. 39). Thus representatives of a genre may be said to resemble each other as siblings do, sharing a number of features in a variety of ways but with no "single feature shared in common by all" (p. 41). A single journal entry may not conform to all of the conventions of the genre and two entries may not share the same features, yet all may have enough features in different combinations to be considered representatives of the genre.

Conventions of the Genre

The teachers of the course in question were not consciously teaching a genre, nor did they lay out all of the conventions of the genre for the students when the class began. Rather they presented the conventions for writing personal journals in a number of implicit and explicit ways during the course. These included oral instructions for in-class and at-home assignments; written assignment sheets from which the students selected topics for their journals; the teachers' own journal entries, which were distributed to the students; the teachers' responses to the students' writing; and classroom materials, particularly an excerpt from Lillian Hellman's memoir, *An Unfinished Woman* (1974), which was presented to the students as a model for their own journal entries.

Through these various means, the teachers encouraged the students to engage in a type of writing characterized by particular functions, content, audience, and organizational and linguistic form. The functions of the writing were both representational (students were encouraged to describe events, people, objects, and issues in their lives) and reflective (they were also asked to reflect on the influences and importance of those events, people, objects, and issues). The content focused on personally significant experiences and feelings of the writers. The audience was primarily the teacher, who most frequently responded to the content rather than the form of the writing and did not "correct" the entries. The organizational form included (1) at the beginning, the identification of time, place, and person(s) involved, and the introduction of the general theme of the entry; (2) a thematically unified central section focused on one event, person, object, or issue; and, (3) at the end, reflection on the meaning or significance of the event, person, object, or issue discussed in the middle. Linguistic features included the predominance of the first-person singular pronoun, use of past tense, and the expression of the writer's thoughts, feelings, and attributes through particular syntactic structures (first-person subject + stative verb + adjective noun: "I was very shy as a child," first-person subject + mental verb + clause or phrase: "I think I feel rejected," and questions). One of the teachers' journal entries, shown in Appendix A, illustrates how these conventions were realized.

Method

The setting for the study was an extended education ESL writing class called Writing for Fluency, which was team-taught one evening a week for two 10-week semesters at San Francisco State University. The primary ongoing writing activity of these classes was the type of personal journal writing described above. For the first 7 weeks of each course, the students wrote nothing but personal journals, selecting three journal topics per week from several possible topics given to them by the teachers (see Vanett & Jurich, Chapter 4, this volume, for a sample assignment). Though a few focused on present or future events in the students' lives, suggested topics primarily directed the students to examine their past from various perspectives—e.g., to give detailed descriptions of significant periods or points in their lives, to explain the significance of an object of importance to them, or to write a portrait of an important person from their past. The students handed in only one of their three weekly journal entries for a teacher's response, so they wrote some entries for no audience other than themselves. They also shared one or two of their entries with other students in peer reading activities. In the last three weeks, the students worked on a final project, which involved the only nonjournal writing of the course. They continued to write weekly journal entries, but the focus of classroom activities shifted to this project, for which they chose the type of writing they would do, e.g., academic essays, business letters, resumés with cover letters, or more personal journals.

The course was developed by Lauren Vanett and Donna Jurich (see Chapters 2 and 4, this volume, for a more detailed description of the course). They designed the class as they did because they had found that many students in their academic writing classes produced more fluent and substantive writing when asked to write about personal experiences than they did in more academic pieces. They believed that by writing about themselves, students would become engaged in communicating through writing, rather than simply trying to fill a predetermined organizational structure with words and sentences to satisfy a teacher's requirements, as often happens in composition classes. Writing would therefore become a more meaningful and less threatening activity for them. The goals for the course were for the students to increase their confidence in their own ideas and their ability to communicate them in written English and, in turn, to become more fluent and competent writers.

One important feature of the class was that each week the teachers wrote and distributed their own journal entries on the same topics that they assigned to the students. They did this for several reasons: to understand the students' writing processes better by writing themselves, to establish a rapport with the students by sharing the writing experience and the content of their journals with them, to model an appropriate degree of intimacy and personal revelation for the journals, and to provide examples of the writing processes and products of native speakers. They did not discuss their journals in class or intend that they be models for the students' writing; they simply gave them to the students each week. Eight of the nine students in this study, however, reported that they considered the teachers' journals to be models as well as interesting reading.

Thirty-eight students, 12 males and 26 females, completed the two classes. Half of them were matriculated university students enrolled in other classes, and the other half were working people who were taking no other classes besides this one. They came from various ethnic and language backgrounds. Most had been in the United States longer than 3 years, some as long as 12 to 15 years. All of them had some experience writing in English, but they took the class—which was voluntary and fulfilled no outside requirements—because they felt themselves to be weak writers in English. Their English fluency was estimated by the teachers to be intermediate.

The subjects for the study consisted of two teachers for each semester (three different teachers altogether because one teacher taught both semesters) and nine students, who served as subjects for case studies. Three of them were from Japan, two from Thailand, and one each from Vietnam, the Philippines, Puerto Rico, and El Salvador. Four of the students were enrolled in other classes as well. The students were selected primarily on the basis of their interest in participating in the study. Since the majority of those interested were females and I wanted to eliminate one of many individual differences (in this case, gender), all of the case study students were females.

I wanted to determine the extent to which students learned and followed in their own journals the conventions that were presented to them and what factors influenced their degree of engagement with the genre. I had four sources of data: a questionnaire that I designed and distributed at the beginning of each semester; field notes, audiotapes, and course materials collected during observations of all 20 class meetings; interviews conducted with teachers and students; and the journals written by both teachers and students.

Findings

Students' Engagement with the Genre

In attempting to determine whether and to what extent students in the class learned the genre conventions they were exposed to, I found that the process of acquiring the genre in order to produce it was quite complex. In addition, in acquiring this genre students had to adapt to being asked to perform this particular task—to produce personal, reflective writing in a classroom context. To understand what the students' behaviors meant as well as what they were, I had to examine their reactions and adaptations to being asked to engage in the genre, as well as the extent to which they followed its conventions in their written texts.

The nine case study students adapted to this genre, which involved them in description of and reflection on their own experiences for an outside audience, in four different ways: by (a) embracing the genre, (b) struggling with audience, (c) developing their own agenda, and (d) escaping the genre. The students' processes were influenced by individual experiences, expectations, and personal and cultural values.

Embracing the genre. One student—Sita, from Thailand—embraced the genre in word and deed. She reported no difficulty with the writing and followed more of the conventions in more of her journals than any other student. Throughout the course, she felt positively about the personal writing she was doing, describing the process as follows: "As I wrote the journal for class, I felt as if I were a weaver who woved the past and present of my life, line after line, in to one tapestry" (Journal #4, 3/26/85).

She realized that she had learned a great deal about herself, not just because of the writing but also because of her stage in life and her experience:

> I think it's a combination, not just the writing [that's caus-ing me to learn so much about myself]. In 1983, I had been through heavy tragedies and I think that really shook me. And maybe my age also; I'm thirty-eight years old now. So it's like everything is just ripe.
>
> (Interview #2, 4/4/85)

Thus Sita believed that her engagement with the genre was enhanced by her life experiences.

Struggling with audience. Five students struggled in different ways with writing about their own experiences for an audience. Raquel, from Puerto Rico, struggled with the personal nature of the writing. Because she had kept a personal journal for 13 years—her "closest companion" in which she had "explored, understood and brought out some of [her] deepest feelings" (Journal #5, 10/7/85)—she was aware of a difference in the degree of personal disclosure she felt comfortable with in her writing for the class and in her own personal journal. She reported that she felt "comfortable" writing about herself in the class, but acknowledged that "some personal things you don't want to com-municate. You have to use vocabulary, not to hide, but to give only some information, not all" (Interview #1, 10/11/85). She used the teachers' journals as models to help her resolve this issue: "The teach-ers' journals show you that you can write about yourself and not be threatened. You can tell significant things without being very per-sonal" (Interview #2, 11/8/85). Raquel struggled with this issue throughout the course and yet was consistently able and willing to engage in the personal, reflective conventions of the genre to a greater degree than were most of the other students (see Appendix B for an example of her journal writing).

Like Raquel, Keiko found the personal nature of the writing diffi-cult, though for different reasons. Keiko had never done much personal writing and did not like to write about herself. In fact, "openness" was an important personal issue for her, one that she had become especially aware of after having lived in the United States for four years and having seen the contrast between Japanese and American cultures. In Japan, she had considered herself "strongly opinionated," which had made her a nonconformist because in Japan "you can't have strong opinion[s]." However, in the United States she found herself to be "very, very Japanese," that is, much less open and assertive about her ideas than most Americans. She felt that she had had "very little self-disclosure" in her life and felt uncertain about describing her own experiences in her journals (Interview #2, 4/11/85). However, her attitudes toward her openness in the journals changed as the class progressed. After a few class sessions, she found that the journal writing was more enjoyable and that she could describe and reflect on her own experience more easily, though she still saw limits to what she could comfortably include in her journal entries.

Keiko's writing bears out many of her perceptions about herself and her writing. The writing did not come easily for her for reasons that she attributed to personal experience and cultural values regarding openness. Yet, in those pieces in which she did more fully engage in the genre, she addressed personally significant content and reflected to a greater extent than many of the other students did in any entries they wrote for the class, and she recognized the benefits of this engagement.

Like Raquel, Kimiko had kept a personal journal in her native language, Japanese, and more recently in English, in which she wrote "to [her] anger or frustration, based on [her] feelings" (Interview #1, 3/8/85). However, Kimiko's reactions to the class and to the writing were greatly influenced by the fact that she was taking another English class simultaneously, a required ESL literature class that she found frustrating, difficult, and useless. In the literature class, she wrote essays "to get my grade" (Interview #1). In contrast, Kimiko found the journal writing "fun." Though she felt it to be harder to express her feelings in English than in Japanese, she said that she was "comfortable" with the writing, which she described as "subjective, writing about our own experience, based on feelings." She also saw the writings as "very personal," but because the assignments gave "a certain direction" to the entries and because the teachers wrote journals for the students to read, she did not find this a serious problem.

After the class had ended and she had completed both courses, making the "conflict" between the two no longer immediate, Kimiko acknowledged that she had some difficulty with the personal, reflective nature of the journal writing: "I enjoy writing the journal, but sometimes I don't want to show my feelings . . . . I hesitated to show my feeling in my journal at first but by the end of the semester, I did it" (Interview #3, 5/17/85). In fact, she showed her feelings and followed the conventions of reflection to a greater extent overall toward the end of the semester than at the beginning. Nevertheless, her difficulty sharing her feelings with an outside audience concerned her less than the fact that she felt more comfortable and less pressured writing about herself and her feelings than being forced to write about short stories that she did not necessarily like or understand.

Kaoru, from Japan, had also kept a personal journal in her native language for approximately 15 years and thus had had experience writing about significant personal experiences and exploring her feelings in writing. She found it more difficult to express her feelings in English than in her native language, and she was aware of the differences between her own personal journal and her journal writing for this class. Unlike Raquel, however, Kaoru focused on more formal differences arising from the existence of an outside audience when comparing the two types of journal writing. Though she described some of the pieces she wrote for the class as "really private," her difficulty with the genre arose not from the personal nature of the writing, but from the fact that she had to use different styles for "private" and "public" writing. She felt that the way she had learned to write in English was inappropriate for private writing because it contained too many complicated sentences and obvious transition words, but that the way she wrote in her Japanese diary was too "emotional" for others to understand. Her goal was to integrate the two styles, to write "logically but also emotionally" (Interview #3, 12/2/85).

From a reader's (and analyst's) perspective, Kaoru succeeded in communicating her experiences and her feelings and reflections about them in her writing class. She consistently followed the genre conventions in a larger proportion of her 11 pieces than did most of the other students. Having written extensively in her own journal about "emotional" events and issues, she seemed to be more familiar than the other students with this personal, reflective genre.

Like Keiko, Irene, who was from Vietnam, had never done much personal writing in her native Chinese or in English, and she had never written about her "feelings" in English before taking the class. Yet she did not find the writing for the class difficult, explaining, "We have a lot to say about our own things" (Interview #1, 10/14/85). Despite reporting no problems with the writing, however, Irene did not follow the conventions of personal content and reflection in as large a proportion of her pieces as the five students mentioned above. Like Kimiko, she did not fully engage in the personal, self-reflective conventions of the genre in her first few pieces, tending instead to describe recent activities and people she had recently seen or met. The first in which she followed most of the conventions were her seventh and eighth entries, in which she described her arrival in the United States after being in a refugee camp and her decision to escape Vietnam by boat when she was 18 years old (see Appendix B for the latter). After those pieces, she wrote 11 more, 6 of which involved a relatively high degree of reflection about significant personal experiences.

Thus, Irene did not report feeling any reluctance to reflect on "personal things." Yet, it took 2 weeks and 6 entries before she did so in her writing. Perhaps, just as Sita's life experience contributed to her readiness to engage in the journal writing to the extent that she did, Irene's life experience, elicited by the assignment to think of significant and meaningful events and transitions in her life, stimulated her willingness and desire to engage in the genre. Having left home and family "to face the edgeless ocean" all alone at 18 (Journal #5, 10/7/85), and having barely survived days on a boat not knowing whether she would ever see her family again, Irene had had experiences that this type of writing allowed her to explore in a way she had never done before. In fact, she said that when she left home she did not cry because she had to pretend to be strong, but that when she wrote about it, she "got some tears" (Interview #3, 11/25/85).

Developing one's own agenda. Two students, Sunee and Alicia, developed their own agendas, following certain conventions while ignoring others. In fact, Sunee, from Thailand, followed fewer of the conventions than any other student and did not usually distinguish this genre from others, such as academic essays, in interviews. She had used English writing only in school and had never written about her own life and feelings before, yet she reported feeling "good" about the writing in the class, partly because "five or ten years later, we can look at it and recall the past" (Interview #1, 10/9/85). She described the writing as "a way to express our feelings, what we feel inside" and said that "the benefit of writing about yourself is to improve your English." But in fact, she did not express her feelings in 71% of her entries, did not include more than three reflective constructions in 43% of them, did not use any questions, and did not write predominantly in the first person singular in 74% of her entries. In interviews as well as in her journal entries, Sunee tended to present herself as a member of a group rather than as an individual, using first-person plural in contexts in which first-person singular would have seemed a more logical choice.

In the piece that she considered the most "important" of those that she wrote for the class, she described a fire that occurred in her neighborhood when she was 12 years old (see Appendix B; note the predominance of first-person plural over first-person singular). She said she thought she had changed as a result of writing the piece:

> Before, I thought it was just a fire and people got frightened. But when I sat down and wrote, I realized that's really scary because I was only twelve years old and we had to escape in the middle of the night.
>
> (Interview #3, 11/15/85)

One interpretation of this response is that, by reflecting and writing about this event, she for the first time became aware of her own individual response to the fire rather than perceiving herself as just another member of the group of "people" involved. Perhaps Sunee's conception of herself as a member of a group made this genre, with its focus on the individual's experiences and feelings, incomprehensible or inconceivable to her. Perhaps because of her apparent tendency, evident in interviews, not to reflect on herself and her experience, the reflection called for by the genre lacked saliency for her. For whatever reason, she typically did not follow the genre conventions, yet she completed the course and felt she benefited from it.

Alicia, from El Salvador, generally followed the conventions calling for personal content, but not those of reflection. When the class began she had never heard the term "journal" and had never taken a writing class. She had written very little in English, primarily business letters and memoranda at work, and she had never "thought of doing this kind of writing before . . ., of writing things that [she] had in [her] mind" (Interview #1, 10/19/85). Yet she quickly developed her own agenda for the writing and followed it throughout the course, consistently writing about significant and personal experiences but avoiding reflection and development of ideas. Her writing resembled a diary with its recitations of activities and feelings more than the reflective journal writing of the teachers' and other students' journals (see Appendix B for an example of her journal writing).

Escaping the genre. Finally, one student—Elizabeth, from the Philippines—tried to follow the conventions at first but ultimately felt the need to escape them by dropping out of the class. At the beginning of the class, she recognized that personal writing in which she "expressed" herself was difficult for her "especially when somebody looks at it," yet she was enjoying the class: "It's fun though. It makes me very nostalgic. I remember fun days, write about happy things from the past" (Interview #1, 10/14/85). This conflict between her feelings that the writing was very personal and therefore difficult and that it was, at the same time, fun and beneficial, continued to be part of

Elizabeth's experience throughout the course. She mentioned her personality as a factor in her reaction to the writing: "I think I've always been hiding things within me, but this helps me to open, helps my well-being. It makes you grow and relate to people what you feel" (Interview #2, 10/28/85).

By the middle of the class, Elizabeth had written six of the seven pieces that she would write for the class. Of those pieces, five were about her own experiences; five had reflection at the end, even though somewhat superficial and clichéd (e.g., "She has influenced me in a lot of ways and I'm very greatful" [Journal #2, 10/7/85]); two addressed content that was highly significant in her life (see Appendix B for one of these entries); and four were predominantly in first-person singular. On the other hand, only one expressed her feelings in more than two or three instances, and in three the amount of reflection was minimal.

The picture here is of a student trying to conform to the conventions of the genre and the teachers' expectation of her, someone who found this personal writing difficult but beneficial, someone who was trying to adapt her own needs and values to the expectations of the course. But she ultimately was not able to do so. She did not attend the 7th, 9th and 10th classes. She decided that she would reveal no more in her writing for the class. She was willing neither to *adopt* the expected conventions nor to *adapt* what she was asked to do so that the writing was not "too personal" for her. Though she tried to follow the conventions despite some discomfort, she ultimately found herself so uncomfortable with the writing that she simply had to stop trying.

Summary. One striking feature of these brief accounts is the variety of factors that seem to have influenced these nine students' ways of adapting to this genre. Raquel, Kaoru, and to a lesser extent Kimiko found the writing easier than other students did because they had kept personal journals. Sita's and Irene's life experiences seem to have especially influenced their adaptation to the genre. Elizabeth, Keiko, Sunee, and Alicia had not engaged in much previous self-reflection in their lives or in writing, which caused them some difficulty with the genre. Keiko attributed some of her difficulty to Japanese cultural values with regard to openness; it is possible that she grew up in a less "open" Japan than did Kimiko and Kaoru, who were 11 years younger than Keiko. All except Sita seem to have found it unusual and therefore somewhat difficult to have an outside audience for personal writing, yet all but Elizabeth settled on an approach that was comfortable and that they perceived as beneficial to the development of their writing abilities.

Effects of Engagement with Classroom Personal
Journal Writing

Despite the differences in the ways these nine students adapted to this genre and the difficulties some of them had in adapting, all of them felt that they had benefited from doing the personal writing. All but Keiko reported that they had gained confidence, and all said that they had benefited in other ways, specifically because they wrote about themselves in their journals. Even Elizabeth, who found the writing ultimately too personal to continue after the sixth class, enthusiastically described her increased confidence in her ability to write in English: "I'm more confident that I can write because I've done all this writing. Because of this class, anytime somebody asks me to write about anything, I'll be able to do it" (Interview #2, 1/28/85). Kaoru similarly described her increased self-confidence, particularly her newly discovered ability to write about any subject: "Before, I insisted on the topic; I got mad if a teacher didn't give me a good topic. But now I can write about anything—a table, a chair, the weather" (Interview #3, 12/2/85).

Irene was especially pleased with her increased self-confidence: "This kind of writing restored my self-confidence. I can write. I need time and practice, but this makes me feel I can write in English . . . . Before, I thought I was stupid. The class taught me everybody can write" (Interview #3, 11/25/85). Alicia reported a similar change in her belief in herself as a writer: "I learned not to be scared when I start writing a letter or anything. I don't get too nervous like before. I have more confidence" (Interview #3, 11/30/85).

Only Keiko did not report feeling more confident as a result of having done the writing in the class, but she, along with all of the others, did find the personal nature of the writing beneficial:

> Since it was a journal, I wrote something I never did in other classes. I'm glad I had the opportunity to write about myself and my thinking . . . .
>
> And then writing is not only just writing on paper using pen. It's really yourself, so it's related to how to live or think about the past, the way you lived, and then change in the future.
>
> So, in those kind of big ways, I think maybe it was very beneficial.
>
> (Interview #3, 5/5/85)

The other eight students made similar comments, for example, about the benefits of "discovering [one]self" (Sita, Interview #3, 5/2/85) and "considering [one]self deeply" (Kimiko, Interview #3, 5/17/85). Even

Raquel, who had previously written extensively in her own journal about the most significant events in her life and included these events in her entries for the class (e.g., her mother's death), gained new "insights" and "realized different things" through her writing for the class. Alicia, who did not reflect on the events she described in her journals, "discovered that when you write, you feel better" and that things "came alive again" for her when she wrote about them (Interview #2, 11/2/85). Finally, Elizabeth found that besides helping her to get ideas, the writing helped her to be more "open" and to "grow" in relating to other people, as well as to recognize changes she had gone through in relation to issues and attitudes she described in her younger life (Interview #2, 10/28/85).

The confidence these students gained made many of them believe in themselves as writers, in their abilities to communicate in written English and improve their writing skills. Without such confidence, many of them were reluctant to take risks and make commitments to writing that could facilitate the development of their writing abilities. Rather than avoiding writing in English, as many of them had previously, they felt ready to take a more aggressive approach to writing. And taking a more active approach, interacting with texts rather than treating them as wholly external to themselves as writers, may make them more likely to learn from writing and to improve their skills no matter what genre they may be writing in (Applebee, 1981, 1984; Langer & Applebee, 1986; Vygotsky, 1962).

Discussion and Pedagogical Implications

Through implicit and explicit means, the teachers in the two classes described presented a written genre with a characteristic set of features of function, audience, form, and content. Most of the nine case study subjects followed some of those conventions in many of their journals. They went through individual processes of adapting to the conventions, processes influenced by previous writing experiences, life experiences, and cultural and personal values vis-à-vis writing about and reflecting on personal experiences. Despite these differences, all nine of the students believed that they had benefited from the writing. These findings can inform educators and educational theorists alike.

First, teachers do not teach and students do not learn writing in a vacuum. Teachers teach genres, that is, certain types of writing with certain features of form, content, use, and audience. They teach students how to "write about particular things in particular ways" (Langer & Applebee, 1986, p. 173). Likewise, students learning a second language or dialect do not learn its formal features in isolation;

they learn the conventions of the discourse genres (both spoken and written) of the group that speaks the language or dialect they are learning.

Just as teachers have become more cognizant in recent years of passing on values and norms through a "hidden curriculum," they need to be aware that they are presenting discourse conventions implicitly as well as explicitly when they teach writing in particular and language in general. Once teachers recognize this fact, they can make conscious decisions about which conventions to teach and how best to teach them. Teachers also need to be alert to the possibility that students may have difficulty because of the conventions of the genre(s) they are asked to engage in, not just because of the linguistic features of the second language they are using. If they recognize the sources of such difficulties, teachers can be more effective in helping students overcome them.

Second, the findings provide further evidence for one fact that teachers already know and struggle with regularly: each student is an individual unlike any other. As difficult as it is, teachers must try to treat students as the individuals they are. Particularly in multicultural classrooms, teachers need to be cautious in their reliance on cultural values and customs to explain students' behavior and learning. Culture may play a role, but individual perceptions, experiences, knowledge, and values may have a greater influence. Though a knowledge of different cultural values can make teachers aware of the influence of culture on individuals, cultural stereotyping can blind them to the myriad of individual experiences, knowledge, and perceptions that students bring to any writing task. It would have been a gross miscalculation, for example, to assume that Sunee, who engaged in fewer genre conventions than any other student, and Sita, who engaged in more of them than any other student, would respond to journal writing similarly because they were both Thai women. To help students who are having difficulty with tasks set for them, teachers need to consider not only or primarily the cultures students come from, but also, to the extent that teachers can learn about them, the individual experiences, knowledge, and values students have brought to the tasks.

The influence of what the individual student brings to the acquisition of genre constitutes one of the many factors that make it "a complex process" (Fowler, 1982). Teachers cannot expect students to learn a genre simply because they tell them what to do in their writing or even because they give them practice with it. The acquisition of genre involves the individual student's previous experience with writing and with the genre as well as his or her life experiences, knowledge, and values. It is also influenced by the type of writing the student is being asked to do, the type of interaction with the teacher in the classroom and as audience for the student's writing, the functions of the writing, and the student's perceptions of and values with regard to those functions. Doubtless there are other influences on the acquisition of genre as well. If they are aware of the complexity of the process and take into account all of these influences, teachers can more successfully help students acquire skill in a genre by addressing their concerns and difficulties and allowing for individual differences in approaches to and engagement with genres.

Individual differences and difficulties may play an equally influential role in students' engagement with other, more common genres than personal journal writing. Teachers have a lot to learn, for example, about students' learning of and engagement with the academic essay, in which they must demonstrate some skill to succeed in educational contexts.

The findings also suggest that audience can strongly influence a student's engagement with a genre. In this study, audience was one of the most salient and troublesome features of the writing for many of the students. This difficulty is largely due to the fact that classroom personal journal writing combines elements of what Goffman (1973) has called "front stage" and "back stage" performances: the audience (teachers), setting (a classroom), and purpose (ultimately to get some evaluation and feedback on their writing performances) call for a "front stage" performance by participants—a performance for the public. The content of the writing (descriptions of and reflection on personal events) is usually reserved for "back stage"—for the performer and selected intimates. The students in this class therefore had to adjust their perceptions of the "context of situation" (Britton et. al., 1975) to the type of writing they were engaged in—personal writing for a teacher.

On the other hand, because the teachers also wrote journals and responded to the students' journals primarily as readers and not as evaluators, most of the students successfully adapted to the genre. Britton et al. (1975) and Applebee (1981) found that the primary type of audience for student writing in British and American secondary schools, respectively, was teacher-as-evaluator, and they argued that students should have other types of audiences for their writing—e.g., collaborators or partners in dialogue. These findings suggest that the audience stance taken by a teacher can be crucial to students' engagement with a genre and therefore that teachers need to make conscious decisions about what audience role(s) they play in response to students' writing. Rather than simply playing the "default" role of evaluator, teachers must practice responding to student writing as interested readers and "collaborators" in learning (Applebee, 1984).

Finally, with regard to personal journal writing in the classroom, an awareness of some of the difficulties that students may have with the genre can help teachers respond in appropriate and effective ways to students' concerns as well as to their writing, allowing them to reflect on personally significant content only to the extent that they are comfortable, for example. Despite these potential difficulties, personal journal writing offers particular benefits that other kinds of classroom writing do not. It can lead students to increased confidence in their abilities to write in English, which in turn can make them more likely to take risks and make commitments to writing that can facilitate the development of their writing abilities. This genre also involves students in reflective thinking, a valuable skill that may carry over to other types of writing. The act of reflecting, of stepping back from what one is writing about to consider one's thoughts and feelings about its content, is a part of the thinking process that is involved in producing most types of writing, including more formal genres. To make a convincing argument, to explain an issue effectively, or to clarify the significance or meaning of events, writers must reflect on the content they are presenting.

Journal writing can be especially beneficial for students who lack confidence in their ability to write (in English) and who lack experience with writing in English. It gives students practice writing in a nonthreatening situation to an audience who responds to what they have communicated rather than to what they have *not* communicated. Curriculum designers and teachers can rest assured that students can benefit from engaging in personal journal writing in the classroom.

References

Applebee, A. N. (1981). *Writing in the secondary school.* Urbana, IL: National Council of Teachers in English.

Applebee, A. N. (1984). *Contexts for learning to write.* Norwood, NJ: Ablex.

Applebee, A. N., & Langer, J. A. (1983). Instructional scaffolding: Reading and writing as natural language activities. *Language Arts 60* (2), 168–175.

Britton, J. (1970). *Language and learning.* London: Penguin Press.

Britton, J., Burgess, T., Martin, N., McLeod, A., & Rosen, H. (1975). *The development of writing abilities (11–18).* London: Macmillan.

Bruner, J.S. (1966). *Toward a theory of instruction.* Cambridge, MA: Harvard University Press.

Ferguson, C. (1986). The study of religious discourse. In D. Tannen and J. E. Alatis (Eds.), *Languages and linguistics: The interdepen-*

dence of theory, data and application (pp. 205–213). Washington, DC: Georgetown University Press.

Fowler, A. (1982). *Kinds of literature: An introduction to the theory of genres and modes.* Cambridge, MA: Harvard University Press.

Goffman, I. (1973). *The presentation of self in everyday life.* Woodstock, NY: Overlook Press. (First published 1959).

Heath, S. B., & Branscombe, A. (1985). "Intelligent writing" in an audience community: Teacher, students and researcher. In S. W. Freedman (Ed.), *The Acquisition of written language: Revision and response* (pp. 49–76). Norwood, NJ: Ablex.

Hellman, L. (1974). *An unfinished woman.* NY: Bantam Books.

Langer, J. A., & Applebee, A. N. (1986). Reading and writing instruction: Toward a theory of teaching and learning. In E. Z. Rothkopf (Ed.), *Review of research in education* (pp. 171–194). Washington, DC: American Educational Research Association.

Martin, N. (Ed.). (1975). *Writing across the curriculum pamphlets.* Upper Montclair, NJ: Boynton/Cook.

Peyton, J. K. (1988). Mutual conversations: Written dialogue as a basis for student-teacher rapport. In J. Staton, R.W. Shuy, J.K. Peyton, & L. Reed, *Dialogue journal communication: Classroom, linguistic, social, and cognitive views* (pp. 183–201). Norwood, NJ: Ablex.

Staton, J. (1988). Contributions of the dialogue journal research to communicating, thinking, and learning. In J. Staton, R.W. Shuy, J. K. Peyton, & L. Reed. *Dialogue journal communication: Classroom, linguistic, social, and cognitive views* (pp. 312–321). Norwood, NJ: Ablex.

Vygotsky, L. S. (1962). *Thought and language* (E. Hanfmann & G. Vakar, Eds. and Trans.). Cambridge, MA: The MIT Press.

Appendix A
Example of a Teacher's Journal

. . . I have several objects which have meaning in my life . . . . The earrings would make an interesting story—better than the medal from my grandmother. So, it is the earrings.

Where should I start? I have to go back seven years, more or less. It was the Christmas before my husband and I separated. We had had a stormy August and September with a lot of fights. Actually, we didn't fight a lot. So, there were a lot of unspoken feelings, anger, frustration, distress. It was the lack of communication that made the two months uneven and upsetting. So, at Christmas, I was not feeling very close to him or very jolly. That was difficult for me because I was (am) a great believer in the spirit of Christmas and do my best to make it a warm caring time. But, our problems and a fight on Christmas Eve made me feel at the bottom of it all. As I sat next to his parents Christmas tree while everyone tore into their gifts, I felt distant, depressed. The last gift passed out was to me. I had failed to notice all evening that I hadn't received a "big" gift from my husband. So, I found a very large box in my hands. I fussed with it hating to open it in front of the whole family and make all the appropriate comments "How lovely! Just right! Thank you Kevin. I love you." I thought it would all stick in my throat. Finally, everyone made me open it. Inside, I found a tiny note saying follow this string. (I had failed to see the string coming out of the box because of all the wrapping paper and general confusion.) The string led me to a small box on the tree. I opened it slowly to find a pair of diamond earrings. I lost my breath and was overwhelmed. I sat, for one of the few times, dumbfounded. You see I had mentioned several years before that I wanted a pair of diamonds knowing then that we were too poor to get them. Kevin had kept that thought and found this pair in May. He had been paying for them little by little, through all our fights and nonfights, so that he could give them to me on Christmas. All the planning, all the secrecy, showed me he cared, yet I knew then that all the planning, all the secrecy, was not enough. Though he had done everything just the way I like it, with all the surprise, with all the magic, with all the love, I knew that we wouldn't last much longer.

Now, you may ask, how could earrings which came with such sadness be favorites of mine? Well, I see those earrings representing care, planning, hard work and secrecy. They remind me of what love can do, of how important planning, hard work and care are in a relationship and for an individual. They also remind me that secrecy and surprises are not always pleasant. What I had kept hidden, my feelings, and what Kevin had kept hidden, the gift, hurt the relationship because it was too late.

So, I wear the earrings whenever I must face a difficult situation. I wear them to give me confidence and to remind me how to act. If I have to go to a meeting I don't like or a party I would rather not go to, I wear the earrings. Then, I know to act what is in my heart with care.

Appendix B
Examples of Student Journals

Raquel
Journal #4, 10/7/85
When I was 21 years of age the most important person in my life, died.

My mother, my sister and I lived in a nice town in my country. Our life was like the life of many working families: my mother worked to support the family and my sister and I studied to be proffesional and to support my mother in her old age. My parents were divorced since I was ten years old. My father never took out the responsabilities I think that as father he should take. Thus, all the family burden leaned over my mother's shoulders. She spent almost all her life working and working hard to give a good education to her two daughters.

When my mother was going to see the fruit of her efforts in terms of our education, she got a cerebral stroke that put her in 5 days of comma. We were not expecting this hit in our lives. Those days were the worse days in my life. My mother was the most important person in my life. She was the meaning of my existence and I was losing that in those days of agony. The feelings I experimented with in those days were unknown for me. I was rebeled with every thing, especially with God. I didn't understand why that was happening to us. She was too young to die. I was totally unable to stop the death and that made me feel angry when I saw my own weakness in front of the death. Even the doctors couldn't do anything.

After five days, my mother died. The following days and months were months of completely loneliness, sadness, and emptiness. Her absence was evident in every moment of my life.

As time went by, I got involved in different activities. The death of my mother left another taste in my life. I started to see the life from another perspective of somebody who had suffered the lose of the beloved one. After that I could understand the suffering of different people because I was sensitive to this. I was alert of when [?] was happening around me and started to rebel against all kinds of injustice, oppresion and suffering.

Irene
Journal #6 10/7/85
In a raining night in 1978, I packed up my cloths, and left my house without saying good bye to anybody. I knew I will never be back again.

I was a stuff decision to make. I didn't want to leave my parents, my brothers, and my grandma, but I didn't have any other alternation either. I was 15 when the Communist took over South Viet Nam in 1975. Since then, my whole life was changed. I changed from a pure and happy young girl, who didn't have anything else to worry bende [besides?] her homework assignments, to a girl who had to live in a scary and worried situation every day and night. I didn't know what the local government really wanted from me. They called me to meetings at least three times a week. They wanted me to become a member of the Communist Party. They wanted me to went to their school. They suggested me to do this , or to do that. I felt totally confuse about my own life and my future. Finally, in one day in the year of 1978, they suggested me to leave my parents and stayed in the dormitory which located far away from the city. They gave me two choices. Either I jointed them volunterrily or they would use force to bring me over there. My family was shocked with this new, and I knew it was time that I had to make a decision. After some careful considerations, I chose to leave my family and escape from the country by boat.

I left my house in the rainning night during the end of October, with the tear drops on the faces of my family. I wanted to cry, really, but I didn't. I had to pretend that I was strong enough to face the furture on my own. Yet, at the bottom of my heart, I was so afraid and confuse to face the edgeless ocean, the uncertain future of myself. I would miss all of my family, my friends, and my little puppy who was grasping my foot and started to cry. Embracing him in my arms, I told my puppy that it was the last time I held him and then we would be separated forever. At 11 o'clock that night, I left my house without a promise to come back. "Mama", I said to my parents as I stepped out the door, "If I unfortually die on the ocean, please forgive me. Please just pretend that you didn't born me, raise me, and I didn't exist in your life at all."

Now, six years had past by. I am still alive, and my family has been reunion. Yet, I never forget that sadness moment in my life. I will never forget my friends, my relatives, and my little pupply who had shared my happiness, my laughter, and my tears.

Sunee
Journal #13, 11/11/85 (Revision of Journals #5, 9 and 10)
It was Sunday morning in the late winter of 1970 and a little while before everyone in my neighborhood could imagine what would happen to them in the next hour. At 2:00 a.m. in the morning when everyone was deeply sleeping, a fire started from a store at the corner about five blocks away from my house. Everyone was awakened by the alarm and started grabbing some valuable things to take along with them in case the fire reached our house.

Most of the houses in my neighborhood were built of weak wood, roofed with poor tiles, and could catch fire easily.

At that time, I lived in an extended family with my uncle, my aunt, their four children, and their son's family; altogether, about twenty-five members were in the household. The three-story house was built by my uncle and my father in the center of Bangkok about fifty years ago. Each family lived in the same household, but we lived on different floors and did our own cooking and housecleaning. The house was filled with warmth and we lived happily. However, it was sold ten years ago when my uncle passed away.

But on that night, the fire expanded and moved rapidly from one building to the next. Everyone gathered whatever he could and stayed away from the house. People gathered outside the house and started to talk about the fire. Everyone had the same question about how it started. At the same time, they were aware of what would happen to the stores nearby, the markets next to them, and the houses in the area. Within five minutes backed up by the winter wind, the fire spread to the next building, followed by the cracking sound of the blaze, the collapse of walls, and the breaking of roofs.

Luckily, the winter wind blew the fire in the direction away from my house, but the whole neighborhood on the opposite side was destroyed. Fifteen minutes later the fire truck arrived with a full tank of water. It was late; all they could do was to spray water onto the next houses, soaking them to slow the coming fire. Two hours later, after a long, heavy fight by the firemen, the fire was gone, but nothing was left. Many people lost their homes, businesses, and properties so they felt depressed.

The next day we felt relief that the fire was over. I went to school as usual. Some of my friends were so happy that we were not one of the victims. No one was surprised when the policemen confirmed that it was an arson fire because the land owner wanted to rebuild the whole area as commercial buildings so that he could earn more money. Since that time, although we could not have prevented that fire, we might have controlled it better if we had been more prepared. Thus, we decided to learn a lot about fire prevention measures.

Alicia
Journal #7, 11/11/85 (Revision of Journals 1 and 5)
I was born and grew up on a farm. When I was five years old my little sister and I had this little house to play with our dolls; we used to stay away from the big house for hours. We also had friends who came over to play. When I reached the age to go to first grade, I was very excited and happy. My parents brought me to school, and I met my teacher Oh! I liked her a lot. But after school; Then was my favorite time. I used to rush home to put on my swimming suit and run down the hill to the river to swim with my sister and friends. From the river I could see the beautiful sun setting behind the big rock. The water of the river was so clean and clear that you could even appreciate the beautiful sunset looking at it in the water. My friends and I also had competitions to see whoever could climb to the highest rock and jump into the water from there. In the morning, after a rainy night even the fruit trees were slippery. I liked to climb them to pick the wet fruit as if it were just washed by somebody, and the birds would sing and sound so happy because soon they were going to start eating the fruit

like I was eating it; I used to eat while I was up in the tree and when my Mom called us for breakfast I was so full already that I almost never could eat my breakfast.

The days that I got so worried were when my mom got sick, and seeing her spending full days in bed, I did not know what to do but cry. After she got better, I felt like every thing was normal, that the sun was shining again in the house. Then I went back to enjoy the beautiful nature again.

Elizabeth
Journal #5, 10/28/85 (Revision of Journal #3)
Inanimate Object
There have been several objects that in one way or another in its own small way have became a part of my life. This particular object that I would like to point out has certainly not only influenced me but reflected my whole religious view. I'm talking about cut-out articles from Bishop Sheen's newspaper column.

. . . My interest started in the early 70's when I was about 15 years old. I was reading a Philippine newspaper when my attention was caught by this column about life in general. I read the whole column and after noting that the writer was Fulton Sheen I immediately agreed w/out any doubt to whatever was stated in that write-up. My conformity was based particularly his being a Bishop laying down guidelines. These were not the only reasons why I started to read & cut-out Bishop Sheen's column everyday. I saw it as a guide in life expressed in a very fine & handsome form almost poetry. Bishop Sheen addresses his theme differently from other religious writers. I think he approaches it very realistically. Being young then, I related to that form. Most of all, it was his way of playing with words that lured me to his writing. There are certainly other writers if not as good maybe even better than Bishop Sheen but for me he is the best. Thereafter, I consistently collect his column in the newspaper and read other books that he has written.

. . . The more I read his writing, the more I adored it and the more I cut it out. Then, all of a sudden, one day, I just cannot find his column but I did not give up looking for it and occasionally I'd find one.

During this time, I decided to take Transidental Mediation (TM) for what reason I cannot recall. I was beginning to attend the TM sessions regularly until such time when I read Sheen's column about his strong dislike and disapproval of this meditation. And because of this I quit the session with out hesitancy. Until now, I'm still pondering, what would be my state of mind at present if I continued doing TM. TM is an exercise of the mind so maybe if I continued doing it today I would have a very sharp perception of things around me, very good concentration and very good ability to analyze things or situations. Despite of these fantasies, I do not regret having quit it and I am happy with my present state of mind.

Sheen's column in the newspaper became scarcer & scarcer until I finally gave up.

Presently, I still have a collection of his writing and I'm very proud of it. I remember showing & sharing it to people close to me that showed interest in him. I had a plan for a long time to put all this collection in an album so I'll be able to keep it forever if I can.

Although at present I do not collect his articles, it still exist in my mind. It must have influenced me in a lot more ways than I can express it. The only thing I'm positive about is that it guided me for the better. Long time no Sheen!

7

Coherence in Deaf Students' Writing

JOHN ALBERTINI

National Technical Institute for the Deaf
Rochester Institute of Technology

Abstract

In this chapter a schema for looking at the internal organization of dialogue journal entries is discussed. It is argued that the entries of three deaf writers are lucid and coherent texts and that classroom teachers can use the dialogue journal writing and the schema presented to foster coherence in students' writing.

Coherence in Deaf Students' Writing

JOHN ALBERTINI

Many people are now trying to become less helpless, both personally and politically: trying to claim more control over their own lives. One of the ways people most lack control over their own lives is through lacking control over words. Especially written words. Words come at you on a piece of paper and you often feel helpless before them. And when you want to put some words of your own back on another piece of paper, you often feel even more helpless. (Elbow, 1973, p. vii)

I doubt that Peter Elbow was thinking of deaf students when he wrote these words. Yet many of my deaf college students express feelings of helplessness and lack of control when faced with typical college writing assignments. To a language teacher, "control" usually means knowledge and correct use of the grammar and vocabulary of that language. For psycholinguists, "control" also implies the ability to consider alternative permutations of words, the ability to consider form as well as content. This ability has been called language objectivity or "metalinguistic awareness" (Hakes, 1980). I suggest here that a writer's awareness of the coherence and organization of a written text is objectivity at the discourse level: discourse objectivity. Secondly, I argue that two deaf writers, while lacking control over specific English structures, nevertheless can write coherent and organized texts. Finally, I suggest that dialogue journals can be used to elicit coherent texts and to show insecure and defeated writers the inherent control and order in their own writing.

Language objectivity, or the ability to regard language as an object—to look at it, analyze it, play with it—is, like the acquisition of language itself, a developmental phenomenon. In preschool children

127

the first signs of objectivity may be the creation and enjoyment of nonsense words. At first, when asked for a long word, French-speaking children will respond with a word like *train*, because it has many cars, or when asked for a small word, will give *primevère* (*primrose*), a small flower. Gradually, children are able to disassociate the word (or phrase) from its object (Papandropoulou & Sinclair, 1974). In the early school years, children begin to appreciate linguistic ambiguity; that is, the fact that words and phrases can have more than one meaning. Witness a first or second grader's delight in riddles and word puns. Other related abilities that develop are the ability to recognize synonymy and the acceptability of sentences solely on the basis of grammatical criteria. These later developments are, not surprisingly, thought to coincide with the development of formal operations (Hakes, 1980). Thus language objectivity, like language, appears to be acquired.

Related to schooling, it has been argued that language objectivity, or metalinguistic awareness, facilitates the acquisition of literacy (Chomsky, 1981; Simons & Murphy, 1986). That is, the greater the ability a student has to manipulate sounds, words, structures, and meanings, the more likely it is that the student will be able to entertain multiple interpretations of a word, sentence, or paragraph. Carol Chomsky (1981) has written and piloted classroom materials that focus the attention of 8-, 9- and 10-year-olds on ambiguity, synonymy, and grammatical acceptability in English.

Beyond the recognition of word- and sentence- level meaning is the ability to recognize clarity or ambiguity at the discourse level. Two factors affecting clarity at this level, and usually mentioned when writing is taught, are coherence and organization. The ability to recognize and produce coherent writing and writing that follows a plan is here taken as discourse objectivity. Following Tannen, "coherence" is taken to mean "the underlying organizing structure making the words and sentences into a unified discourse . . ." (1984, p. xiv). With older students who are able to deal with much longer chunks of language, dialogue journals may be the medium in which to practice discourse objectivity.

Dialogue journal writing, by definition, offers a measure of control to the student. Unlike other academic journals or sketchbooks, the medium is interactive and involves maintaining a meaningful conversation over a specified time period, an objective. Because teacher and student are partners in dialogue, the student can select and discard topics at will. Suggestions from the teacher to expand on a certain topic may or may not be heeded. So, when a student writes at length on a topic, it means either that she knows something about it or that she is genuinely interested in it. The degree to which students become aware of their ability to exercise this kind of control in an interactive situation varies, yet most realize the possibilities early on. However, the kind of control that I discuss here is one that most students are not aware of: that is, the control over the structure—the coherence and organization—of one's discourse.

The Given-New Contract

One way to discuss coherence and organization in written text is in terms of the "given-new contract." Once defined, this conceptual schema will be used to analyze the dialogue journal entries of two deaf writers.

The "given-new contract" refers to an expectation, hypothesized for listeners and readers of English, that the speaker or writer will generally present old or given information before new. It has been shown that readers' comprehension time is faster (Clark & Haviland, 1977) and that recall is faster and more accurate (Vande Kopple, 1982) when text conforms to the given-new sequence. In an earlier study, Stinson and Albertini (1985) found that colleagues asked to select "coherent" sentence alternatives for short paragraphs regularly selected those alternatives that conformed to the given-new sequence over those that did not. Weissberg (1984) analyzed 60 paragraphs taken from published experimental research reports in agriculture, biology, and engineering, the kind his English as a second language graduate students were required to read. Following the patterns of topic development outlined by Daneš (1974), Weissberg found that, in paragraphs where patterning occurred, the most common pattern was the "linear" version of the given-new sequence. This is where the new information of one sentence is reiterated as the given information in the following sentence.

In his example in Figure 1, underlined words represent the given information. The boxes in the figure are intended to show information in slots—for each sentence there are two, a topic slot (T) and a comment slot (C). The arrows indicate the structural connections or cohesion that is established when C1 is reiterated in T2, C2 in T3, and so on. The second pattern that predominated in Weissberg's samples was the "constant topic progression" (Figure 2), where essentially the same topic is reiterated throughout. The third, the "hypertheme pattern," (Figure 3) is essentially a "parts of the whole" organizational schema, where one facet or part of the whole becomes the topic of each successive sentence. A fourth pattern found in his samples was, not surprisingly, a mixture of the three. Weissberg looked only at the introductory and concluding paragraphs of his sample or experimental reports.

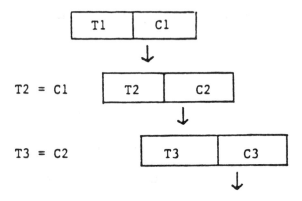

Figure 1.   Linear progression.
Example:
Hydrology is based on the water cycle, more commonly called the hydrologic cycle. *This cycle* can be visualized as beginning with the evaporation of water from oceans and continent lands. *The resulting vapor* condenses to form clouds, which in turn results in precipitated water. *The precipitation* which then falls upon the land is dispersed in several ways . . . . (from a student paper)
Note. From "Given and new: Paragraph Development Models from Scientific English" by R. C. Weissberg, 1984, *TESOL Quarterly, 18,* 485–500. Reprinted by permission.

At the paragraph level, all patterns conform to the given-new contract. They differ as to which unit of information the writer chooses to topicalize. In the "constant topic progression," the same unit of information is the topic of each sentence; in the "linear progression," the "new" unit in each sentence becomes the topic, or the "given," of the next.

Given-New Information in Dialogue Journal Entries

Are the schemas developed by Daneš and Weissberg to describe formal academic writing general enough to apply to informal writing and to the writing of students learning English as a second language? To explore this question, I asked two colleagues for "interesting and coherent" journal entries that their students had written. The selection was random in that neither knew what kind of analysis I had in mind. The following long entry was written by SF, Bonnie Meath-Lang's student.

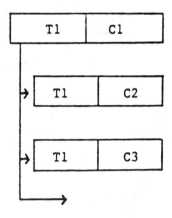

Figure 2.   Constant topic progression.
   Example:
Herbage of crested wheat grass was harvested from 10 unfertilized permanent plots and 10 permanent plots annually fertilized with 8 pounds of nitrogen per acre. *Herbage* from 48 square feet, obtained by hand clipping with a 10' x 12' treatment area was sampled on May 15 (young yield) and on August 1 (mature yield). *The selected herbage* was oven dried in a forced air dryer and the weights were recorded. *Herbage yield and its response to clipping* have been reported elsewhere.
               (from *Journal of Range Management*, 1977, *30*(4), 271)
   Note. From "Given and New: Paragraph Development Models from Scientific English" by R.C. Weissberg, 1984, *TESOL Quarterly, 18*, 485–500. Reprinted by permission.

When I was born, I couldn't walked, talked and moved around. The reason why was that because I was born Cele-bral Palsy. My whole family were very depressing. They were told I would be retarding and won't be able to move around at all and also should send me to a special hospital and to stay there all my life.

One day, my parents took me to many differents kinds of doctors to find out if this doctor can be able to help me out. They finally found a right doctor that said, "Oh, I can help your daughter to walk, talk and move around" & "She would not become like a retarding person." My whole family were praying to God that I would be able to walk.

Six years later, I started to learn how to walk, talk, and crawl on the floor. My parents have been working so hard on me. They took me to the Physical Theaphy everday and

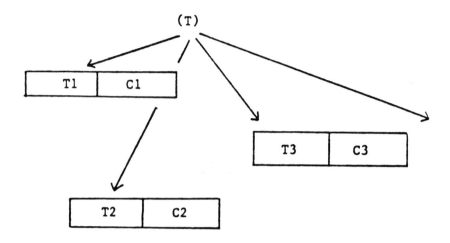

Figure 3.   Hypertheme pattern.
   Example:
The reflector was protected from the weather by an outer window of 0.10 mm tedlar. *The forcal length of the reflector* was 22.8 cm. *The back of the reflector* was protected from the weather with a black polyethylene cover stapled to the frame. *The reflector rack* was mounted as a free standing unit, facing south.

(from Solar Energy, 1977, 19, 395)

   Note. From "Given and New: Paragraph Development Models from Scientific English" by R. C. Weissberg, 1984, *TESOL Quarterly, 18*, 485–500. Reprinted by permission.

---

to the doctor too. We have moved to _____ from _____ . The reason why we move to _____ because there was a very good school for me to go. This school is called "Celebral Palsy Center." This school helped me a lot with speech and everything. When I was up to 14 years old, I left from C.P. center to _____ School for the Deaf. All of sudden, I went to a public school. I disliked _____ because it was too easy for me especially I didn't like to sign language. I am oral and always talk all years long. I mean that I always use my speech all the time. I am hard of hearing.

   I am very proud of myself especially to my parents and family. They are so happy to have me because they have a friend that their son had the same problem as me but he is still mentally retarding and sent to a special hospital (home).

> I am very proud to have a wonderful wisest parents!!
> Some of the parents always listen what the doctor said then
> put their child away. My parents are not that kind of people.
> They have more warm sweet hearts. I really cherish them
> very much. Now I am like a normal person.

Consider the relation of the first two sentences. The topic of the first
sentence is the writer herself ("I"), and the comment is "I couldn't
walked, talked and moved around." The topic of the subsequent sentence ("The reason why . . .") refers back to her physical limitations,
establishing a clear link between the two sentences. Another example
of this kind of link occurs in the third paragraph: "The reason why we
moved to _____ because there was a very good school for me to
go. This school is called . . . ." The information in the comment slot,
"a very good school," is reiterated as the topic of the subsequent
sentence, "This school."

These are examples of what Daneš called linear progression in text.
Much more prevalent in SF's entry, however, is a constant topic progression. From the third sentence of the first paragraph to the end of
the second paragraph, the topic of each sentence is the writer's family.
Linear connections appear in the third and fourth paragraphs as well,
but here, too, the preferred progression is that of constant topic (either
"I" or "my parents").

Whereas SF's journal entry is autobiographical, DS's entry was
written as a personal reaction to a short essay on masks by Rainer
Maria Rilke. Another colleague, Carol Cuneo, frequently invites her
students to respond to thought-provoking poems or essays in the
course of the semester's journal writing.

> The faces are all over the world but we see only mask. Only
> people see their faces, are their relationship or close friend.
> Face is the most important. Face is a isolation. Mask is good
> safe keeping. It stayed out from people and it protect from
> the face. Mask is not authentic, it lie to people. Faces are
> beautiful and natural. Also mask is natural but may not be
> beautiful. Face go through their touch natural world life
> with the mask from the birth till die.

This entry might be paraphrased as:

> Faces are all over the world, but we see only masks. The
> only people who see our faces are relatives or close friends.
> A face is more important. A face is isolation [unique]. A
> mask is good safe-keeping. It stands before people and it
> protects the face. A mask is not authentic; it lies to people.
> Faces are beautiful and natural. Also a mask is natural, but

may not be beautiful. Faces go through experiences in the world and in life with the masks from birth until death.

At first glance the organizational schema seems to be reiteration of a constant topic: first faces, then masks. Each sentence begins with one or the other, and in the first and last sentences faces are mentioned in connection with masks. This implies that faces and masks are different aspects of a single persona. So viewed, the entry falls into the parts-to-whole or hypertheme pattern.

The structural anomalies in this entry are word- and sentence-level anomalies only. Beyond these, and when viewed through the perspective of the given-new contract, a well-organized text emerges. Brevity, simplicity, and adherence to a single organizational schema make this a coherent text.

Conclusion

I have used the given-new contract schema to analyze coherence and organization in two written texts. As Weissberg (1984) pointed out, if the schemas derived from this contract accurately account for a substantial proportion of authentic paragraphs, then teachers have a powerful tool for describing and modeling paragraph development for their students. I have analyzed two dialogue journal entries written by English learners who were focusing on content (often personal), not on written form. The writers have adhered closely to one or more organizational schemas. Beyond the obvious surface anomalies in these students' English is clear evidence of coherence and order in their presentation of information.

The awareness that students *can* produce coherent, organized text even if they have not yet mastered surface linguistic markers is important for teachers as they attempt to help students develop their writing abilities. This awareness is also important for students themselves. As teachers write to students in dialogue journals, they can help to develop this awareness in their students. I am suggesting neither that teachers tamper with journal entries in the form of correcting, nor that they teach these schemas and make students self-conscious when writing journal entries. What I am suggesting is that teachers can respond to students on two levels. First and foremost, they should respond honestly to the information presented. This alone validates the written product and, indirectly, the students' experiences and ideas. Second, teachers can respond to the way students have said something—to the order of their text. Below is an exchange in which the teacher responds in the second way.

Teacher: There is a lot of powerful feeling in your description about you and your brother. I got lost in one
place though. All of a sudden your relationship
changed (beginning with the sentence "And then
Tom taught me everything. . .). What happened
between this sentence and the previous one to
change your relationship?

JD: . . . About my brother and me. I hope you will find
your way out.

At the time we hate each other, my brother
didn't really wanted to bother me. He just wanted
to be with his friends. And I wanted to be with
them. So I bothered my brother. I joined in myself
by playing games with them . . . in the summer.
We played basketball, 'Who's afraid of the lion,'
football and many others. My brother and I used
to be teamed up together. Sometime we played
against each other, like I was on one team and he
was on the other team. We always played one
on one in basketball. Somehow, I guess playing
game together brought us together. We became
close. Then Tom started teaching me.

Teacher: Thanks for the clarification about your brother.
Your description now makes more sense, and it
is a realistic description of how a personal relationship can change. I hope you will use this description as "raw material" for the next composition. (Albertini & Meath-Lang, 1986, pp. 178–
179.)

In this case, a break in cohesion was easily repaired by the addition
of one or two sentences. In dialogue journals, I suspect most breaks
can be identified and repaired without the specific teaching of organizational schemas. In the "genre" of journal writing (Lucas, Chapter 6,
this volume), it is possible for the teacher simply to comment on the
"tightness," "clarity," and "power" of a student's writing. On the other
hand, more formal analysis and reworking of entries might be appropriate when they are presented to a larger audience; for example,
when they are "published" within the classroom (Vanett & Jurich,
Chapter 2, this volume).

Perhaps because his attention was on content rather than form, JD
was pleasantly surprised when the teacher mentioned the coherence
of his entry. Such comments may foster discourse objectivity or control over one's discourse, which, as Elbow implied, is what teachers

of writing want to give students. In dialogue journals, control over words is not confused with control over experience. In this "genre," students are encouraged to write freely and purposefully about their experiences. Once they have recorded their experience, making an entry or series of entries coherent may be simply a matter of adding either information, as in JD's entry, or appropriate linguistic markers. Viewed in this way, coherence as such is not taught; rather, its expression in conventional terms is practiced.

References

Albertini, J., & Meath-Lang, B. (1986). An analysis of student-teacher exchanges in dialogue journal writing. *Journal of Curriculum Theorizing, 7*(1), 153–201.

Chomsky, C. (1981, October). *Looking at language: A child's eye view.* Paper presented at New York State English for Speakers of Other Languages and Bilingual Education Association Conference, Rochester, NY.

Clark, H., & Haviland, S. (1977). Comprehension and the given-new contract. In R. Freedle (Ed.), *Discourse production and comprehension* (pp. 1–40). Norwood, NJ: Ablex.

Daneš, F. (1974). Functional sentence perspective and the organization of text. In F. Daneš (Ed.), *Papers on functional sentence perspective.* Prague: Academy Publishing House, Czech Academy of Science.

Elbow, P. (1973). *Writing without teachers.* New York: Oxford University Press.

Hakes, D. (1980). *The development of meta-linguistic abilities in children.* New York: Springer-Verlag.

Papandropoulou, I., & Sinclair, H. (1974). What is a word? Experimental studies of children's ideas on grammar. *Human Development, 17*(4), 241–258.

Simons, H. & Murphy, S. (1986). Spoken language strategies and reading acquisition. In J. Cook-Gumperz (Ed.), *The social construction of literacy* (pp. 185–206). New York: Cambridge University Press.

Stinson, M., & Albertini, J. (1985). Summarization skills and linguistic skills in reading text: Suggestions for instruction. *Teaching English to Deaf and Second-language Students, 3*(1), 9–16.

Tannen, D. (1984). *Coherence in spoken and written discourse.* Norwood, NJ: Ablex.

Vande Kopple, W. (1982). Functional sentence perspective, composition, and reading. *College Composition and Communication, 33*(1), 50–63.

Weissberg, R. (1984). Given and new: Paragraph development models from scientific English. *TESOL Quarterly, 18*, 485–500.

Contributors

John Albertini conducts research and teaches at the National Technical Institute for the Deaf. His main research interests are the processing and acquisition of English by American deaf students and the acquisition of German and writing by German deaf students.

Donna Jurich, assistant director of the American Language Institute at San Francisco State University (SFSU), develops materials and techniques that promote student autonomy and interest in writing. As a curriculum writer, teacher trainer, and teacher, she has been exploring the writing process with nonnative English speakers since 1979. She presents regularly at educational conferences and has led workshops on how to teach nonnative speakers in native speaker classrooms. She is also cofounder of the English Fluency Program at SFSU Extended Education, where she teaches and consults part time.

Tamara Lucas is educational equity specialist at the Southwest Center for Educational Equity in Oakland, California. She works with school districts to improve the education of minority students, focusing particularly on literacy instruction for limited-English-proficient students. An ESL teacher since 1979, she has also conducted research on the language and literacy learning of elementary, high school, and adult ESL students.

Bonnie Meath-Lang is chair of technical and integrative communication studies at the National Technical Institute for the Deaf. She has taught writing since 1972 to deaf, nonnative-English-speaking, and adult students, and has done research on the relationship of journal and biographical writing to curriculum and teaching. She spent a semester teaching and consulting in a new bilingual deaf education program at the University of Leeds, West Yorkshire, England.

Joy Kreeft Peyton is a research associate at the Center for Applied Linguistics. She has studied the interactive writing of native and nonnative English speakers, hearing and deaf, in elementary through college settings. A previous high school and adult ESL teacher, she has worked closely with teachers to develop and study various approaches to interactive writing, both in dialogue journals and on computer networks.

Lauren Vanett is the director of the English Fluency Program at San

Francisco State University Extended Education, which she cofounded in 1985. As both teacher and administrator, she develops innovative courses for nonnative English speaking adults that emphasize student and teacher empowerment. She has taught adults in university, community college, and basic education programs, and is a regular presenter at educational conferences and teacher training workshops.

Margaret Walworth has been teaching English at Gallaudet University since 1969. In addition to being the coordinator of the English Department's Tutorial Service, she is chair of the TEDS (Teaching English to Deaf Students) Interest Section of TESOL.